Legal Notice

This book is copyright 2015 with all rights reserved. It is illegal to copy, distribute, or create derivative works from this book in whole or in part or to contribute to the copying, distribution, or creating of derivative works of this book.

ISBN-13: 978-1522856719
ISBN-10: 1522856714

BOOKS FROM THE GET 800 COLLECTION FOR COLLEGE BOUND STUDENTS

28 SAT Math Lessons to Improve Your Score in One Month
>   Beginner Course
>   Intermediate Course
>   Advanced Course

320 SAT Math Problems Arranged by Topic and Difficulty Level

320 SAT Math Subject Test Problems Arranged by Topic and Difficulty Level
>   Level 1 Test
>   Level 2 Test

The 32 Most Effective SAT Math Strategies

SAT Prep Official Study Guide Math Companion

SAT Vocabulary Book

320 ACT Math Problems Arranged by Topic and Difficulty Level

320 AP Calculus AB Problems Arranged by Topic and Difficulty Level

320 AP Calculus BC Problems Arranged by Topic and Difficulty Level

555 Math IQ Questions for Middle School Students

555 Advanced Math Problems for Middle School Students

555 Geometry Problems for High School Students

Algebra Handbook for Gifted Middle School Students

CONNECT WITH DR. STEVE WARNER

www.facebook.com/SATPrepGet800

www.youtube.com/TheSATMathPrep

www.twitter.com/SATPrepGet800

www.linkedin.com/in/DrSteveWarner

www.pinterest.com/SATPrepGet800

plus.google.com/+SteveWarnerPhD

28 New SAT Math
Lessons to Improve Your Score in One Month

Intermediate Course

For Students Currently Scoring Between
500 and 600 in SAT Math

Dr. Steve Warner

© 2015, All Rights Reserved
SATPrepGet800.com © 2013

Table of Contents

ACTIONS TO COMPLETE BEFORE YOU READ THIS BOOK

1. Purchase a TI-84 or equivalent calculator

It is recommended that you use a TI-84 or comparable calculator for the SAT. Answer explanations in this book will always assume you are using such a calculator.

2. Take a practice SAT from the Official Guide to get your preliminary SAT math score

Your score should be at least a 500. If it is lower, you should begin with the Beginner book in this series.

3. Claim your FREE bonuses

Simply visit the following webpage and enter your email address to receive solutions to all the supplemental problems in this book and other materials.

www.thesatmathprep.com/28Les500.html

4. 'Like' my Facebook page

This page is updated regularly with SAT prep advice, tips, tricks, strategies, and practice problems. Visit the following webpage and click the 'like' button.

www.facebook.com/SATPrepGet800

INTRODUCTION
STUDYING FOR SUCCESS

*T*his book was written specifically for the student currently scoring between a 500 and 600 in SAT math. Results will vary, but if you are such a student and you work through the lessons in this book, then you will see a substantial improvement in your score.

This book has been cleverly designed to enforce the study habits that I constantly find students ignoring despite my repeated emphasis on how important they are. Many students will learn and understand the strategies I teach them, but this is not enough. This book will force the student to internalize these strategies so that the appropriate strategy is actually used when it is needed. Most students will attempt the problems that I suggest that they work on, but again, this is not enough. All too often students dismiss errors as "careless" and neglect to redo problems they have answered incorrectly. This book will minimize the effect of this neglect.

The book you are now reading is self-contained. Each lesson was carefully created to ensure that you are making the most effective use of your time while preparing for the SAT. The initial lessons are quite focused ensuring that the reader learns and practices one strategy and one topic at a time. In the beginning the focus is on Level 1, 2 and 3 problems, and little by little Level 4 problems will be added into the mix. It should be noted that a score of 700 can usually be attained without ever attempting a Level 5 problem. That said, some Level 5 problems will appear late in the book for those students that show accelerated improvement. The reader of this book should not feel obligated to work on these harder problems the first time they go through this book.

There are two math sections on the SAT: one where a calculator is allowed and one where it is not. I therefore recommend trying to solve as many problems as possible both with and without a calculator. If a calculator is required for a specific problem it will be marked with an asterisk (*).

1. Using this book effectively

- Begin studying at least three months before the SAT.
- Practice SAT math problems ten to twenty minutes each day.
- Choose a consistent study time and location.

You will retain much more of what you study if you study in short bursts rather than if you try to tackle everything at once. So try to choose about a twenty minute block of time that you will dedicate to SAT math each day. Make it a habit. The results are well worth this small time commitment. Some students will be able to complete each lesson within this ten to twenty minute block of time. Others may take a bit longer. If it takes you longer than twenty minutes to complete a lesson, you have two options. You can stop when twenty minutes are up and then complete the lesson the following day, or you can finish the lesson and then take a day off from SAT prep that week.

- Every time you get a question wrong, **mark it off, no matter what your mistake**.
- Begin each lesson by first redoing the problems from previous lessons on the same topic that you have marked off.
- If you get a problem wrong again, **keep it marked off**.

As an example, before you begin the third "Heart of Algebra" lesson (Lesson 9), you should redo all the problems you have marked off from the first two "Heart of Algebra" lessons (Lessons 1 and 5). Any question that you get right you can "unmark" while leaving questions that you get wrong marked off for the next time. If this takes you the full twenty minutes, that is okay. Just begin the new lesson the next day.

Note that this book often emphasizes solving each problem in more than one way. Please listen to this advice. The same question is never repeated on any SAT (with the exception of questions from the experimental sections) so the important thing is learning as many techniques as possible. Being able to solve any specific problem is of minimal importance. The more ways you have to solve a single problem the more prepared you will be to tackle a problem you have never seen before, and the quicker you will be able to solve that problem. Also, if you have multiple methods for solving a single problem, then on the actual SAT when you "check over" your work you will be able to redo each problem in a different way. This will eliminate all "careless" errors on the actual exam. Note that in this book the quickest solution to any problem will always be marked with an asterisk (*).

2.   Calculator use.

- Use a TI-84 or comparable calculator if possible when practicing and during the SAT.
- Make sure that your calculator has fresh batteries on test day.
- You may have to switch between DEGREE and RADIAN modes during the test. If you are using a TI-84 (or equivalent) calculator press the MODE button and scroll down to the third line when necessary to switch between modes.

Below are the most important things you should practice on your graphing calculator.

- Practice entering complicated computations in a single step.
- Know when to insert parentheses:
  - Around numerators of fractions
  - Around denominators of fractions
  - Around exponents
  - Whenever you actually see parentheses in the expression

Examples:

We will substitute a 5 in for x in each of the following examples.

Expression	Calculator computation
$\dfrac{7x+3}{2x-11}$	$(7*5 + 3)/(2*5 - 11)$
$(3x-8)^{2x-9}$	$(3*5 - 8)^\wedge(2*5 - 9)$

9

- Clear the screen before using it in a new problem. The big screen allows you to check over your computations easily.
- Press the **ANS** button (**2ND (-)**) to use your last answer in the next computation.
- Press **2ND ENTER** to bring up your last computation for editing. This is especially useful when you are plugging in answer choices, or guessing and checking.
- You can press **2ND ENTER** over and over again to cycle backwards through all the computations you have ever done.
- Know where the $\sqrt{\ }$, π, and ^ buttons are so you can reach them quickly.
- Change a decimal to a fraction by pressing **MATH ENTER ENTER**.
- Press the **MATH** button - in the first menu that appears you can take cube roots and nth roots for any n. Scroll right to **NUM** and you have **lcm(** and **gcd(**.
- Know how to use the **SIN**, **COS** and **TAN** buttons as well as **SIN^{-1}**, **COS^{-1}** and **TAN^{-1}**.

You may find the following graphing tools useful.

- Press the **Y=** button to enter a function, and then hit **ZOOM 6** to graph it in a standard window.
- Practice using the **WINDOW** button to adjust the viewing window of your graph.
- Practice using the **TRACE** button to move along the graph and look at some of the points plotted.
- Pressing **2ND TRACE** (which is really **CALC**) will bring up a menu of useful items. For example selecting **ZERO** will tell you where the graph hits the x-axis, or equivalently where the function is zero. Selecting **MINIMUM** or **MAXIMUM** can find the vertex of a parabola. Selecting **INTERSECT** will find the point of intersection of 2 graphs.

3. Tips for taking the SAT

Each of the following tips should be used whenever you take a practice SAT as well as on the actual exam.

Check your answers properly: When you go back to check your earlier answers for careless errors *do not* simply look over your work to try to catch a mistake. This is usually a waste of time.

- When "checking over" problems you have already done, **always redo the problem from the beginning** without looking at your earlier work.
- If possible use a different method than you used the first time.

For example, if you solved the problem by picking numbers the first time, try to solve it algebraically the second time, or at the very least pick different numbers. If you do not know, or are not comfortable with a different method, then use the same method, but do the problem from the beginning and do not look at your original solution. If your two answers do not match up, then you know that this is a problem you need to spend a little more time on to figure out where your error is.

This may seem time consuming, but that is okay. It is better to spend more time checking over a few problems, than to rush through a lot of problems and repeat the same mistakes.

Take a guess whenever you cannot solve a problem: There is no guessing penalty on the SAT. Whenever you do not know how to solve a problem take a guess. Ideally you should eliminate as many answer choices as possible before taking your guess, but if you have no idea whatsoever do not waste time overthinking. Simply put down an answer and move on. You should certainly mark it off and come back to it later if you have time.

Pace yourself: Do not waste your time on a question that is too hard or will take too long. After you have been working on a question for about 1 minute you need to make a decision. If you understand the question and think that you can get the answer in another 30 seconds or so, continue to work on the problem. If you still do not know how to do the problem or you are using a technique that is going to take a long time, mark it off and come back to it later if you have time.

Feel free to take a guess. But you still want to leave open the possibility of coming back to it later. Remember that every problem is worth the same amount. Do not sacrifice problems that you may be able to do by getting hung up on a problem that is too hard for you.

Attempt the right number of questions: There are two math sections on the SAT – one where a calculator is allowed and one where a calculator is not allowed. The calculator section has 30 multiple choice (mc) questions and 8 free response (grid in) questions. The non-calculator section has 15 multiple choice (mc) questions and 5 free response (grid in) questions.

You should first make sure that you know what you got on your last SAT practice test, actual SAT, or actual PSAT (whichever you took last). What follows is a general goal you should go for when taking the exam.

Score	MC (Calculator Allowed)	Grid In (Calculator Allowed)	MC (Calculator Not Allowed)	Grid In (Calculator Not Allowed)
< 330	10/30	3/8	4/15	1/5
330 – 370	15/30	4/8	6/15	2/5
380 – 430	18/30	5/8	8/15	2/5
440 – 490	21/30	6/8	9/15	3/5
500 – 550	24/30	6/8	11/15	4/5
560 – 620	27/30	7/8	13/15	4/5
630 – 800	30/30	8/8	15/15	5/5

For example, a student with a current score of 530 should attempt 24 multiple choice questions and 6 grid ins from the section where a calculator is allowed, and 11 multiple choice questions and 4 grid in questions from the section where a calculator is not allowed.

This is *just* a general guideline. Of course it can be fine-tuned. As a simple example, if you are particularly strong at Algebra problems, but very weak at Geometry and Trig problems, then you may want to try every Algebra problem no matter where it appears, and you may want to reduce the number of Geometry and Trig problems you attempt.

Grid your answers correctly: The computer only grades what you have marked in the bubbles. The space above the bubbles is just for your convenience, and to help you do your bubbling correctly.

Never mark more than one circle in a column or the problem will automatically be marked wrong. You do not need to use all four columns. If you do not use a column just leave it blank.

The symbols that you can grid in are the digits 0 through 9, a decimal point, and a division symbol for fractions. Note that there is no negative symbol. So answers to grid-ins *cannot* be negative. Also, there are only four slots, so you cannot get an answer such as 52,326.

Sometimes there is more than one correct answer to a grid-in question. Simply choose one of them to grid-in. *Never* try to fit more than one answer into the grid.

If your answer is a whole number such as 2451 or a decimal that only requires four or less slots such as 2.36, then simply enter the number starting at any column. The two examples just written must be started in the first column, but the number 16 can be entered starting in column 1, 2 or 3.

Note that there is no zero in column 1, so if your answer is 0 it must be gridded into column 2, 3 or 4.

Fractions can be gridded in any form as long as there are enough slots. The fraction 2/100 must be reduced to 1/50 simply because the first representation will not fit in the grid.

Fractions can also be converted to decimals before being gridded in. If a decimal cannot fit in the grid, then you can simply *truncate* it to fit. But you must use every slot in this case. For example, the decimal .167777777… can be gridded as .167, but .16 or .17 would both be marked wrong.

Instead of truncating decimals you can also *round* them. For example, the decimal above could be gridded as .168. Truncating is preferred because there is no thinking involved and you are less likely to make a careless error.

Here are three ways to grid in the number $\frac{8}{9}$.

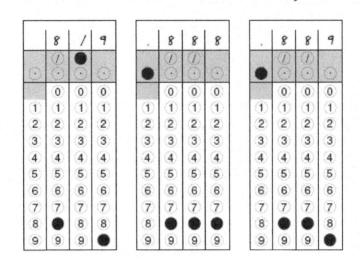

Never grid-in mixed numerals. If your answer is $2\frac{1}{4}$, and you grid in the mixed numeral $2\frac{1}{4}$, then this will be read as $\frac{21}{4}$ and will be marked wrong. You must either grid in the decimal 2.25 or the improper fraction $\frac{9}{4}$.

Here are two ways to grid in the mixed numeral $1\frac{1}{2}$ correctly.

14

LESSON 1
HEART OF ALGEBRA

Start with Choice (B) or (C)

In many SAT math problems you can get the answer simply by trying each of the answer choices until you find the one that works. Unless you have some intuition as to what the correct answer might be, then you should always start in the middle with choice (B) or (C) as your first guess (an exception will be detailed in the next strategy below). The reason for this is simple. Answers are usually given in increasing or decreasing order. So very often if choice (B) or (C) fails you can eliminate one or two of the other choices as well.

Try to answer the following question using this strategy. **Do not** check the solution until you have attempted this question yourself.

LEVEL 1: HEART OF ALGEBRA

1. If $7 + x + x = 3 + x + x + x$, what is the value of x ?

    (A) 1
    (B) 2
    (C) 3
    (D) 4

Solution by starting with choice (C): We start with choice (C) and substitute 3 in for x on each side of the equation.

$$7 + 3 + 3 = 3 + 3 + 3 + 3$$
$$13 = 12$$

Since this is false, we can eliminate choice (C). A little thought should allow you to eliminate choices (A) and (B) as well (don't worry if you don't see this – just take another guess). Let's try choice (D) next.

$$7 + 4 + 4 = 3 + 4 + 4 + 4$$
$$15 = 15$$

Thus, the answer is choice (D).

Before we go on, try to solve this problem in two other ways.

(1) Algebraically (the way you would do it in school).
(2) By "striking off $x's$."

Here is a hint for method (2):

Hint: If the same expression appears as a **term** on each side of an equation, you can simply cross out each of these expressions, and the equation remains "balanced."

Algebraic solution: Here is a quick algebraic solution to the problem.

$$7 + x + x = 3 + x + x + x$$
$$7 + 2x = 3 + 3x$$
$$7 = 3 + x$$
$$4 = x$$

Thus, the answer is choice (D).

Remark: We can begin with an algebraic solution, and then switch to the easier method. For example, we can write $7 + 2x = 3 + 3x$, and then start substituting in the answer choices from here. This will take less time than the first method, but more time than the algebraic method.

* (2) Striking off $x's$: When the same term appears on each side of an equation we can simply delete that term from both sides. In this problem we can strike off two $x's$ from each side to get

$$7 = 3 + x.$$

This becomes $4 = x$, choice (D).

When NOT to Start with Choice (B) or (C)

If the word **least** appears in the problem, then start with the smallest number as your first guess. Similarly, if the word **greatest** appears in the problem, then start with the largest number as your first guess.

Try to answer the following question using this strategy. **Do not** check the solution until you have attempted this question yourself.

16

LEVEL 1: HEART OF ALGEBRA

2. For which of the following values of k will the value of $11k - 12$ be greater than 21?

   (A) 1
   (B) 2
   (C) 3
   (D) 4

* Solution by starting with choice (D): Since the word **greater** appears in the problem let's start with the largest number for our first guess. This is choice (D).

$$11k - 12 = 11 \cdot 4 - 12 = 44 - 12 = 32.$$

Since 32 is greater than 21, the answer is choice (D).

Before we go on, try to solve this problem algebraically (without using the answer choices).

Algebraic solution:
$$11k - 12 > 21$$
$$11k > 33$$
$$k > 3$$

The only answer choice with a number greater than 3 is choice (D).

You're doing great! Let's just practice a bit more. Try to solve each of the following problems by using one of the two strategies you just learned. Then, if possible, solve each problem another way. The answers to these problems, followed by full solutions are at the end of this lesson. **Do not** look at the answers until you have attempted these problems yourself. Please remember to mark off any problems you get wrong.

LEVEL 1: HEART OF ALGEBRA

3. If $5(x - 7) = 4(x - 8)$, what is the value of x?

   (A) 1
   (B) 2
   (C) 3
   (D) 4

17

4. If $4^2 = 2^z$, then $z =$

    (A) 4
    (B) 3
    (C) 2
    (D) 1

5. If $3c + 2 < 11$, which of the following CANNOT be the value of c ?

    (A) 0
    (B) 1
    (C) 2
    (D) 3

$$\frac{5 + \Delta}{2} = 8\frac{1}{2}$$

6. What number, when used in place of Δ above, makes the statement true?

    (A) 4
    (B) 5
    (C) 9
    (D) 12

LEVEL 2: HEART OF ALGEBRA

7. * If $6^{x+1} = 7776$, what is the value of x ?

    (A) 6
    (B) 5
    (C) 4
    (D) 3

18

LEVEL 3: HEART OF ALGEBRA

8. There is the same number of cows, pigs and chickens being transported to a farm. When the transport arrives at the farm, 4 cows are taken off the truck and 8 chickens are placed on the truck. If there are now twice as many pigs as cows on the truck, and twice as many chickens as pigs on the truck, how many chickens are on the truck?

    (A) 6
    (B) 8
    (C) 12
    (D) 16

Definitions Used in This Lesson

$x < y$ means "x is less than y."
For example, $2 < 3$ and $-4 < 0$ are TRUE, whereas $6 < 5$ is FALSE.

$x > y$ means "x is greater than y."
For example, $3 > 2$ and $0 > -4$ are TRUE, whereas $5 > 6$ is FALSE.

It sometimes helps to remember that for $<$ and $>$, the symbol always points to the smaller number.

Answers

1. D	5. D
2. D	6. D
3. C	7. C
4. A	8. D

Full Solutions

3.

Solution by starting with choice (C): We start with choice (C) and substitute 3 in for x in the given equation.

$$5(x - 7) = 4(x - 8)$$
$$5(3 - 7) = 4(3 - 8)$$
$$5(-4) = 4(-5)$$
$$-20 = -20$$

Thus, the answer is choice (C).

* Algebraic solution:

$$5(x - 7) = 4(x - 8)$$
$$5x - 35 = 4x - 32$$
$$x = 3$$

Thus, the answer is choice (C).

Note: To get from the first to the second equation we used the distributive property on each side of the equation. This property will be covered in detail in Lesson 7.

 4.

Solution by starting with choice (C): First note that $4^2 = 16$. Now let's begin with choice (C). We substitute 2 in for z to get that $2^z = 2^2 = 4$. This is too small so we can eliminate choices (C) and (D). We next try choice (B). We substitute 3 in for z to get $2^z = 2^3 = 8$. This is still too small so we can eliminate choice (B). The answer must therefore be (A). We should still check that it works. We substitute 4 in for z and we get $2^z = 2^4 = 16$. So the answer is indeed choice (A).

* Direct solution: $4^2 = 16 = 2^4$. So $z = 4$. Thus, the answer is (A).

 5.

Solution by starting with choice (D): We start with choice (D) and substitute 3 in for c in the given inequality.

$$3c + 2 < 11$$
$$3(3) + 2 < 11$$
$$9 + 2 < 11$$
$$11 < 11$$

Since this is FALSE, the answer is choice (D).

* Remark: This is actually a slight variation of the second strategy. A moment's thought should tell you that we are looking for a number that is too big. So the largest number given must be the answer.

Algebraic solution:

$$3c + 2 < 11$$
$$3c < 9$$
$$c < 3$$

Thus, the answer is choice (D).

6.

Solution by starting with choice (C): We start with choice (C) and substitute 9 in for Δ in the given equation.

$$\frac{5+9}{2} = 8\frac{1}{2}$$
$$\frac{14}{2} = 8\frac{1}{2}$$
$$7 = 8\frac{1}{2}$$

The equation is false. So we can eliminate choices (A), (B), and (C). So the answer must be choice (D). Let's verify this. We substitute 12 for Δ.

$$\frac{5+12}{2} = 8\frac{1}{2}$$
$$\frac{17}{2} = 8\frac{1}{2}$$
$$8\frac{1}{2} = 8\frac{1}{2}$$

So yes, the answer is choice (D).

* Algebraic solution:

$$\frac{5+Δ}{2} = 8\frac{1}{2}$$
$$5 + Δ = 17$$
$$Δ = 12$$

This is choice (D).

7.

Solution by starting with choice (C): We start with choice (C) and substitute 4 in for x in the given equation. We type in our calculator $6\^(4 + 1) = 7776$. Thus, the answer is choice (C).

Calculator note: Instead of typing $6\^(4 + 1)$ in our calculator, we can add 4 and 1 in our head (to get 5), and type $6\^5$ instead.

* Algebraic solution: We rewrite the equation so that each side has the same base (in this case the common base is 6). $6^{x+1} = 6^5$. Now that the bases are the same, so are the exponents. Thus, $x + 1 = 5$, and therefore $x = 4$, choice (C).

8.

Solution by starting with choice (B): If there are 8 chickens, then there are 4 pigs, and 2 cows. That means there were originally 0 chickens, 4 pigs, and 6 cows. Since these numbers are not equal we can eliminate choice (B), and choice (A) as well.

Let's try choice (C) next. If there are 12 chickens, then there are 6 pigs, and 3 cows. That means there were originally 4 chickens, 6 pigs, and 7 cows. Again, these numbers are not equal so we can eliminate (C).

Let's verify that the answer is choice (D). If there are 16 chickens, then there are 8 pigs, and 4 cows. That means there were originally 8 of each. So the answer is choice (D).

* Algebraic solution: Let x be the original number of chickens (so x is also the original number of pigs, and the original number of cows). We then have

$$x = 2(x - 4) \quad \text{and} \quad x + 8 = 2x$$

Each of these equations has the unique solution $x = 8$. So the number of chickens is

$$x + 8 = 8 + 8 = 16, \text{ choice (D)}.$$

Caution: Before choosing your answer always double check what the question is asking for. In this case we must find the number of chickens which is $x + 8$, **not** x.

Detailed formal solutions of the above two equations:

$$
\begin{array}{ll}
x = 2(x - 4) & \quad x + 8 = 2x \\
x = 2x - 8 & \quad 8 = x \\
-x = -8 & \\
x = 8 &
\end{array}
$$

OPTIONAL MATERIAL

Informal and Formal Algebra

Suppose we are asked to solve for x in the following equation:

$$x + 3 = 8$$

In other words, we are being asked for a number such that when we add 3 to that number we get 8. It is not too hard to see that $5 + 3 = 8$, so that $x = 5$.

I call the technique above solving this equation **informally**. In other words, when we solve algebraic equations informally we are solving for the variable very quickly in our heads. I sometimes call this performing **"mental math."**

We can also solve for x **formally** by subtracting 3 from each side of the equation:

$$\begin{array}{rl} x + 3 &= 8 \\ -3 & -3 \\ \hline x &= 5 \end{array}$$

In other words, when we solve an algebraic equation formally we are writing out all the steps – just as we would do it on a test in school.

To save time on the SAT you should practice solving equations informally as much as possible. And you should also practice solving equations formally – this will increase your mathematical skill level.

Let's try another:

$$5x = 30$$

Informally, 5 times 6 is 30, so we see that $x = 6$.

Formally, we can divide each side of the equation by 5:

$$\begin{array}{c} \dfrac{5x}{5} = \dfrac{30}{5} \\ x = 6 \end{array}$$

Now let's get a little harder:

$$5x + 3 = 48$$

We can still do this informally. First let's figure out what number plus 3 is 48. Well, 45 plus 3 is 48. So $5x$ is 45. So x must be 9.

Here is the formal solution:

$$5x + 3 = 48$$
$$\underline{-3 \quad -3}$$
$$\underline{5x \quad = 45}$$
$$\underline{5 \qquad 5}$$
$$x \quad = 9$$

Now practice some on your own. Try to solve each of the following equations for x both informally, and formally. The answers are below:

1. $x + 17 = 20$
2. $6x = 24$
3. $\frac{x}{12} = 2$
4. $7x - 4 = 24$
5. $\frac{2x-3}{5} = 2$
6. $5(x - 7) = 40$
7. $2^x = 8$
8. $\frac{5+x}{2} = 8\frac{1}{2}$
9. $5^{x+1} = 125$
10. $3^x + 4 = 31$

Answers

1. 3	6. 15
2. 4	7. 3
3. 24	8. 12
4. 4	9. 2
5. 13/2 or 6.5	10. 3

Download additional solutions for free here:

www.thesatmathprep.com/28Les500.html

LESSON 2
GEOMETRY

Turn to page 15 and review **Start with choice (B) or (C).** Then try to answer the following question using this strategy. **Do not** check the solution until you have attempted this question yourself.

LEVEL 1: GEOMETRY

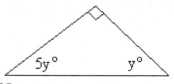

Note: Figure not drawn to scale.

1. In the right triangle above, what is the value of y

    (A) 15
    (B) 18
    (C) 21
    (D) 30

Solution by starting with choice (B): Recall that a triangle has angle measures that sum to 180 degrees, and begin by looking at choice (B). So we let $y = 18$. Then $5y = (5)(18) = 90$.

$$90 + 18 + 90 = 198.$$

Since $198 > 180$ we can eliminate choice (B), as well as choices (C) and (D). So the answer muct be choice (A).

Note: It's a good idea to make sure that choice (A) works. If we let $y = 15$, then $5y = (5)(15) = 75$.

$$90 + 15 + 75 = 180$$

So we have verified that choice (A) is the correct answer.

Before we go on, try to solve this problem algebraically.

* Algebraic solution: $5y + y$ must be equal to 90. So $6y = 90$, and therefore $y = \dfrac{90}{6} = 15$, choice (A).

Turn to page 16 and review **When NOT to start with choice (B) or (C).** Then try to answer the following question using this strategy. **Do not** check the solution until you have attempted this question yourself.

LEVEL 3: GEOMETRY

2. The sum of the areas of two squares is 85. If the sides of both squares have integer lengths, what is the least possible value for the length of a side of the smaller square?

   (A) 1
   (B) 2
   (C) 6
   (D) 7

* Solution by starting with choice (A): Begin by looking at choice (A) since it is the smallest. If the side length of the smaller square is 1, then the area of the smaller square is $1 \cdot 1 = 1$. So the area of the larger square is $85 - 1 = 84$. Since 84 is not a perfect square, we can eliminate choice (A).

Let's try choice (B) next. If the side length of the smaller square is 2, then the area of the smaller square is 4, and the area of the larger square is $85 - 4 = 81$. Since 81 is a perfect square, the answer is choice (B).

Remark: If it is not clear to you that 84 is not a perfect square and a calculator is allowed for the problem, take the square root of 84 in your calculator. You will get approximately 9.16515. Since this is not an integer, 84 is not a perfect square.

81 is a perfect square however because $81 = 9^2$. Again, if this is not clear to you, simply take the square root of 81 in your calculator.

You're doing great! Let's just practice a bit more. Try to solve each of the following problems by using one of the two strategies we just reviewed. Then, if possible, solve each problem another way. The answers to these problems, followed by full solutions are at the end of this lesson. **Do not** look at the answers until you have attempted these problems yourself. Please remember to mark off any problems you get wrong.

LEVEL 1: GEOMETRY

3. If the degree measures of the three angles of a triangle are 100°, $z°$, and $z°$, what is the value of z ?

   (A) 80
   (B) 70
   (C) 60
   (D) 40

4. What is the radius of a circle whose circumference is π?

   (A) $\frac{1}{2}$

   (B) 1

   (C) $\frac{\pi}{2}$

   (D) π

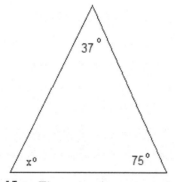

Note: Figure not drawn to scale.

5. In the triangle above, $x =$

   (A) 62
   (B) 64
   (C) 66
   (D) 68

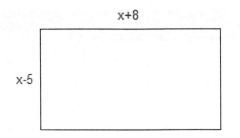

6. If the perimeter of the rectangle above is 78, what is the value of *x*?

    (A) 20
    (B) 19
    (C) 18
    (D) 17

LEVEL 2: GEOMETRY AND TRIG

7. A rectangle has a perimeter of 16 meters and an area of 15 square meters. What is the longest of the side lengths, in meters, of the rectangle?

    (A) 3
    (B) 5
    (C) 10
    (D) 15

LEVEL 3: GEOMETRY

8. The volume of a right circular cylinder is 343π cubic centimeters. If the height and base radius of the cylinder are equal, what is the base radius of the cylinder?

    (A) 3 centimeters
    (B) 5 centimeters
    (C) 7 centimeters
    (D) 15 centimeters

Definitions Used in This Lesson

The **integers** are the counting numbers together with their negatives.

$$\{\dots, -4, -3, -2, -1, 0, 1, 2, 3, 4, \dots\}$$

The **positive integers** consist of the positive numbers from that set.

$$\{1, 2, 3, 4, \dots\}$$

A **perfect square** is an integer that is equal to the square of another integer. For example, 9 is a perfect square because $9 = 3^2$.

A **triangle** is a two-dimensional geometric figure with three sides and three angles. The sum of the degree measures of all three angles of a triangle is 180.

A **quadrilateral** is a two-dimensional geometric figure with four sides and four angles. The sum of the degree measures of all four angles of a quadrilateral is 360.

A **rectangle** is a quadrilateral in which each angle is a right angle. That is, each angle has 90 degrees.

A **square** is a rectangle with four equal sides.

A **circle** is a two-dimensional geometric figure formed of a curved line surrounding a center point, every point of the line being an equal distance from the center point. This distance is called the **radius** of the circle. The **diameter** of a circle is the distance between any two points on the circle that pass through the center of the circle.

A **cylinder** is a three-dimensional geometric solid bounded by two equal parallel circles and a curved surface formed by moving a straight line so that its ends lie on the circles.

Formulas Used in This Lesson

The sum of the measures in degrees of the angles of a triangle is 180.
The sum of the measures in degrees of the angles of a quadrilateral is 360.
Perimeter of a rectangle is $P = 2l + 2w$
Area of a rectangle is $A = lw$
Area of a square is $A = s^2$
Circumference of a circle is $C = 2\pi r$
Volume of a cylinder is $V = \pi r^2 h$

Answers

1. A	5. D
2. B	6. C
3. D	7. B
4. A	8. C

Full Solutions

3.

Solution by starting with choice (C): Recall that a triangle has angle measures that sum to 180 degrees, and begin by looking at choice (C). If we take a guess that $z = 60$, then the sum of the angles is equal to $100 + z + z = 100 + 60 + 60 = 220$ degrees. This is too large. We can therefore eliminate choices (A), (B), and (C). The answer is therefore choice (D).

Note: Let us verify that choice (D) works. If $z = 40$ it follows that the sum of the angle measures is $100 + z + z = 100 + 40 + 40 = 180$ degrees. Since this is correct, the answer is choice (D).

* Algebraic solution: A triangle has angle measures that sum to 180 degrees, so we solve the following equation.

$$100 + z + z = 180$$
$$100 + 2z = 180$$
$$2z = 80$$
$$z = 40$$

Therefore the answer is choice (D).

4.

Solution by starting with choice (C): The circumference of a circle is $C = 2\pi r$. Let's start with choice (C) as our first guess. If $r = \frac{\pi}{2}$, then $C = 2\pi\left(\frac{\pi}{2}\right) = \pi^2$. Since this is too big we can eliminate choices (C) and (D).

Let's try choice (B) next. If $r = 1$, then $C = 2\pi(1) = 2\pi$, still too big.

The answer must therefore be choice (A). Let's verify this. If $r = \frac{1}{2}$, then $C = 2\pi\left(\frac{1}{2}\right) = \pi$. So the answer is indeed choice (A).

* Algebraic solution: We use the circumference formula $C = 2\pi r$, and substitute π in for C.

$$C = 2\pi r$$
$$\pi = 2\pi r$$
$$\frac{\pi}{2\pi} = r$$
$$\frac{1}{2} = r$$

This is choice (A).

    5.

Solution by starting with choice (C): Recall that a triangle has angle measures that sum to 180 degrees, and begin by looking at choice (C). If we let $x = 66$, then $66 + 37 + 75 = 178$. This is a bit too small, so we can eliminate choices (A), (B), and (C).

Let's verify choice (D) is correct. If $x = 68$, we get $68 + 37 + 75 = 180$. So the answer is choice (D).

* Algebraic solution: We solve the following equation.

$$x + 37 + 75 = 180$$
$$x + 112 = 180$$
$$x = 68$$

This is answer choice (D).

    6.

Solution by starting with choice (C): Recall that we get the **perimeter** of a rectangle by adding up all four sides. Let's start with choice (C) as our first guess, so that $x = 18$. It then follows that $x - 5 = 18 - 5 = 13$ and $x + 8 = 18 + 8 = 26$. It follows that the perimeter of the rectangle is $13 + 13 + 26 + 26 = 78$. Therefore the answer is choice (C).

Algebraic solution: We solve the following equation.

$$P = 2l + 2w$$
$$78 = 2(x + 8) + 2(x - 5)$$
$$78 = 2x + 16 + 2x - 10$$
$$78 = 4x + 6$$
$$72 = 4x$$
$$\frac{72}{4} = x$$
$$18 = x$$

This is answer choice (C).

7.

* Solution by starting with choice (C): Let's start with choice (C) and guess that the longest side of the rectangle is 10 meters long. But then the length of the two longer sides of the rectangle adds up to 20 meters which is greater than the perimeter. So we can eliminate (C) and (D).

Let's try choice (B) next. So we are guessing that the longest side of the rectangle is 5 meters long. Since the perimeter is 16, it follows that the shortest side must have length 3 (see Remark (1) below for more clarification). So the area is $(5)(3) = 15$. Since this is correct, the answer is choice (B).

Remarks: (1) If one side of the rectangle has a length of 5 meters, then the opposite side also has a length of 5 meters. Since the perimeter is 16 meters, this leaves $16 - 5 - 5 = 6$ meters for the other two sides. It follows that a shorter side of the rectangle has length $\frac{6}{2} = 3$ meters.

(2) When guessing the longest side of the rectangle we can use the area instead of the perimeter to find the shortest side. For example, if we guess that the longest side is 5, then since the area is 15 it follows that the shortest side is 3. We would then check to see if we get the right perimeter. In this case we have $P = 2(5) + 2(3) = 16$ which is correct.

Algebraic solution: We are given that $2x + 2y = 16$ and $xy = 15$. If we divide each side of the first equation by 2, we get $x + y = 8$. Subtracting each side of this equation by x, we get $y = 8 - x$.

We replace y by $8 - x$ in the second equation to get $x(8 - x) = 15$. Distributing the x on the left yields $8x - x^2 = 15$. Subtracting $8x$ and adding x^2 to each side of this equation gives us $0 = x^2 - 8x + 15$. The right hand side can be factored to give $0 = (x - 5)(x - 3)$. So we have $x - 5 = 0$ or $x - 3 = 0$. So $x = 5$ or $x = 3$. Since the question asks for the longest of the side lengths, the answer is $x = 5$, choice (B).

Note: Here is a picture for extra clarification.

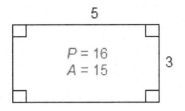

8.

Solution by starting with choice (C): Let's start with choice (C), so that $r = 7$. Then $h = 7$ too. So $V = \pi r^2 h = \pi(7)^2(7) = 343\pi$. This is correct, and so the answer is choice (C).

* Algebraic solution:

$$V = \pi r^2 h$$
$$343\pi = \pi r^2 r$$
$$343 = r^3$$
$$7 = r.$$

Therefore the answer is choice (C).

OPTIONAL MATERIAL

The following questions will test your understanding of formulas used in this lesson. These are **not** SAT questions.

1. Find the perimeter and area of a rectangle with each of the following lengths and widths.

$\ell = 3$, $w = 5$ $\ell = 2.3$, $w = 1.7$ $\ell = x - 2$, $w = x + 3$ $\ell = x - 4$, $w = x^2 + 5$

2. Find the perimeter of a square with area 49.

3. Find the area of a square with perimeter 48.

4. Find the area of a rectangle with perimeter of 100 and length 20.

5. Find the perimeter of a rectangle with area 35 and width 7.

6. Find the area of a rectangle with perimeter 100.

Answers

1. $P = 16$, $A = 15$; $P = 8$, $A = 3.91$; $P = 4x + 2$, $A = (x − 2)(x + 3) = x^2 + x − 6$; $P = 2x^2 + 2x + 2$, $A = (x − 4)(x^2 + 5) = x^3 − 4x^2 + 5x − 20$

2. $4(7) = 28$

3. $(48/4)^2 = 12^2 = 144$

4. $w = (100 − 2(20))/2 = (100 − 40)/2 = 60/2 = 30$. So $A = (20)(30) = 600$

5. $\ell = 35/7 = 5$. So $P = 2(5) + 2(7) = 10 + 14 = 24$.

6. **Cannot be determined from the given information!** For example in question 4 we saw that A can be 600. But, for example, if $\ell = 10$, then $w = (100 − 2(10))/2 = (100 − 20)/2 = 80/2 = 40$. So $A = (10)(40) = 400$.

Download additional solutions for free here:

www.thesatmathprep.com/28Les500.html

LESSON 3
PASSPORT TO ADVANCED MATH

Functions

A function is simply a rule that for each "input" assigns a specific "output." Functions may be given by equations, tables or graphs.

Note about the notation $f(x)$: The variable x is a placeholder. We evaluate the function f at a specific value by substituting that value in for x. For example, if $f(x) = x^3 + 2x$, then

$$f(-2) = (-2)^3 + 2(-2) = -8 - 4 = -12$$

LEVEL 1: ADVANCED MATH

$$f(x) = 5x + 3$$
$$g(x) = x^2 - 5x + 2$$

1. The functions f and g are defined above. What is the value of $f(10) - g(5)$?

* Solution: $f(10) = 5(10) + 3 = 50 + 3 = 53$

$g(5) = 5^2 - 5(5) + 2 = 25 - 25 + 2 = 2$.

Therefore $f(10) - g(5) = 53 - 2 = \mathbf{51}$.

Now try to answer the following questions about functions. The answers to these questions, followed by full solutions are at the end of this lesson. **Do not** look at the answers until you have attempted these problems yourself. Please remember to mark off any problems you get wrong.

LEVEL 1: ADVANCED MATH

2. For the function $f(x) = 5x^2 - 7x$, what is the value of $f(-3)$?

x	$p(x)$	$q(x)$	$r(x)$
1	5	6	11
2	−3	7	−10
3	−4	−7	3
4	−5	−7	−2
5	−6	0	5

3. The table above gives some values of the functions p, q, and r. At which value of x does $q(x) = p(x) + r(x)$?

LEVEL 2: ADVANCED MATH

$$k(x) = \frac{3}{7}x + c$$

4. In the function above, c is a constant. If $k(14) = 11$, what is the value of $k(-7)$?

$$h(x) = |x^2 - 3| + 2$$

5. For what value of x is $h(x)$ equal to 0?

    (A) 0
    (B) 1
    (C) $\sqrt{3}$
    (D) There is no such value of x

6. Suppose that $h(x) = 4x - 5$ and $h(b) = 17$. What is the value of b ?

    (A) 4
    (B) 5.5
    (C) 10
    (D) 17.5

7. Let a function of 2 variables be defined by $h(x, y) = x^2 + 3xy - (y - x)$. What is the value of $h(5,4)$?

36

LEVEL 3: ADVANCED MATH

8. Let h be a function such that $h(x) = |3x| + c$ where c is a constant. If $h(2) = -3$, what is the value of $h(-4)$?

Answers

1. 51   5. D
2. 66   6. B
3. 4   7. 86
4. 2   8. 3

Full Solutions

2.
* $f(-3) = 5(-3)^2 - 7(-3) = 5(9) + 21 = 45 + 21 = \mathbf{66}$.

Notes: (1) The exponentiation was done first, followed by the multiplication. Addition was done last. See the table below for more information on order of operations.

(2) To square a number means to multiply it by itself. So

$$(-3)^2 = (-3)(-3) = 9.$$

(3) If a calculator is allowed, we can do the whole computation in our calculator in one step. Simply type $5(-3)^\wedge 2 - 7(-3)$ ENTER. The output will be 66.

Make sure to use the minus sign and not the subtraction symbol in front of the 3. Otherwise the calculator will give an error.

Order of Operations: Here is a quick review of order of operations.

PEMDAS	
P	Parentheses
E	Exponentiation
M	Multiplication
D	Division
A	Addition
S	Subtraction

37

Note that multiplication and division have the same priority, and addition and subtraction have the same priority.

3.

* Solution by starting with 3: The answer is an integer between 1 and 5 inclusive (these are the x-values given). So let's start with $x = 3$ as our first guess. From the table $p(3) = -4$, $q(3) = -7$, and $r(3) = 3$. Therefore $p(3) + r(3) = -4 + 3 = -1$. This is not equal to $q(3)$ so that 3 is **not** the answer.

Let's try $x = 4$ next. From the table $p(4) = -5$, $q(4) = -7$, and $r(4) = -2$. So $p(4) + r(4) = -5 + (-2) = -7 = q(4)$. Therefore the answer is **4**.

* Quick solution: We can just glance at the rows quickly and observe that in the row corresponding to $x = 4$, we have $-5 + (-2) = -7$. Thus, the answer is **4**.

4.

* $k(14) = \frac{3}{7}(14) + c = 6 + c$. Since we are given that $k(14) = 11$, we have $6 + c = 11$, and so $c = 11 - 6 = 5$.

So $k(x) = \frac{3}{7}x + 5$, and therefore $k(-7) = \frac{3}{7}(-7) + 5 = -3 + 5 = 2$.

5.

Solution by starting with choice (C): We start with choice (C) and compute $h(\sqrt{3}) = |(\sqrt{3})^2 - 3| + 2 = |3 - 3| + 2 = 0 + 2 = 2$.

So we can eliminate choice (C).

Let's try (B): $h(1) = |1^2 - 3| + 2 = |1 - 3| + 2 = |-2| + 2 = 4$.

So we can eliminate choice (B).

Let's try (A): $h(0) = |-3| + 2 = 3 + 2 = 5$.

So we can eliminate choice (A) and the answer is choice (D).

* Direct solution: $|x^2 - 3| \geq 0$ no matter what x is. It follows that $|x^2 - 3| + 2 \geq 2$.

In particular $|x^2 - 3| + 2$ could never be 0, and so the answer is (D).

Recall: $|x|$ is the **absolute value** of x. If x is nonnegative, then $|x| = x$. If x is negative, then $|x| = -x$ (in other words, if x is negative, then taking the absolute value just eliminates the minus sign). For example, $|12| = 12$ and $|-12| = 12$.

6.

Solution by starting with choice (C): Let's start with choice (C) and guess that $b = 10$. Then $h(b) = 4b - 5 = 4(10) - 5 = 40 - 5 = 35$. This is too big. So we can eliminate choices (C) and (D).

Let's try choice (B) next. So we are guessing that $b = 5.5$. We then have that $h(b) = 4b - 5 = 4(5.5) - 5 = 22 - 5 = 17$. This is correct. So the answer is choice (B).

 * **Algebraic solution:** $h(b) = 17$ is equivalent to $4b - 5 = 17$. We add 5 to each side of this equation to get $4b = 22$. We then divide each side of this equation by 4 to get that $b = 5.5$, choice (B).

7.
* $h(5,4) = 5^2 + 3(5)(4) - (4 - 5) = 25 + 60 - (-1) = 85 + 1 = \textbf{86}$.

Notes: (1) Everywhere we see an x we replace it by 5 and everywhere we see a y we replace it by 4. Remember to follow the correct order of operations (see the solution to problem 2 in this lesson).

(2) We can do the whole computation in our calculator (if allowed) in one step. Simply type $5^2 + 3 * 5 * 4 - (4 - 5)$ ENTER. The output will be 86.

8.
* $h(2) = |3(2)| + c = 6 + c$. But it is given that $h(2) = -3$. So $6 + c = -3$, and therefore $c = -9$. So $h(x) = |3x| - 9$. Finally,

$$h(-4) = |3(-4)| - 9 = |-12| - 9 = 12 - 9 = \textbf{3}.$$

OPTIONAL MATERIAL

Direct Variation

The following are all equivalent ways of saying the same thing:

(1) y varies directly as x
(2) y is directly proportional to x
(3) $y = kx$ for some constant k
(4) $\frac{y}{x}$ is constant
(5) the graph of $y = f(x)$ is a nonvertical line through the origin.

For example, in the equation $y = 5x$, y varies directly as x. Here is a partial table of values for this equation.

x	1	2	3	4
y	5	10	15	20

Note that we can tell that this table represents a direct relationship between x and y because $\frac{5}{1} = \frac{10}{2} = \frac{15}{3} = \frac{20}{4}$. Here the **constant of variation** is 5.

Here is a graph of the equation.

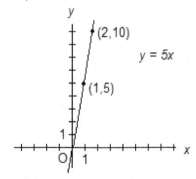

Note that we can tell that this graph represents a direct relationship between x and y because it is a nonvertical line through the origin. The constant of variation is the slope of the line, in this case $m = 5$.

Example: If y varies directly as x and $y = 3$ when $x = 7$, then what is y when $x = 21$?

Solution 1: Since y varies directly as x, $y = kx$ for some constant k. We are given that $y = 3$ when $x = 7$, so that $3 = k(7)$, or $k = \frac{3}{7}$. Thus, $y = \frac{3x}{7}$. When $x = 21$, we have $y = \frac{3(21)}{7} = \mathbf{9}$.

Solution 2: Since y varies directly as x, $\frac{y}{x}$ is a constant. So we get the following ratio: $\frac{3}{7} = \frac{y}{21}$. Cross multiplying gives $63 = 7y$, so that $y = \mathbf{9}$.

Solution 3: The graph of $y = f(x)$ is a line passing through the points $(0, 0)$ and $(7, 3)$. The slope of this line is $\frac{3-0}{7-0} = \frac{3}{7}$. Writing the equation of the line in slope-intercept form we have $y = \frac{3}{7}x$. As in solution 1, when $x = 21$, we have $y = \frac{3(21)}{7} = \mathbf{9}$.

* Solution 4: To get from $x = 7$ to $x = 21$ we multiply x by 3. So we have to also multiply y by 3. We get $3(3) = \mathbf{9}$.

Inverse Variation

The following are all equivalent ways of saying the same thing:

(1) y varies inversely as x
(2) y is inversely proportional to x
(3) $y = \frac{k}{x}$ for some constant k
(4) xy is constant

The following is a consequence of (1), (2) (3) or (4).

(5) The graph of $y = f(x)$ is a hyperbola.

Note: (5) is not equivalent to (1), (2), (3) or (4).

For example, in the equation $y = \frac{12}{x}$, y varies inversely as x. Here is a partial table of values for this equation.

x	1	2	3	4
y	12	6	4	3

Note that we can tell that this table represents an inverse relationship between x and y because $(1)(12) = (2)(6) = (3)(4) = (4)(3) = 12$. Here the **constant of variation** is 12.

41

Here is a graph of the equation. On the left you can see the full graph. On the right we have a close-up in the first quadrant.

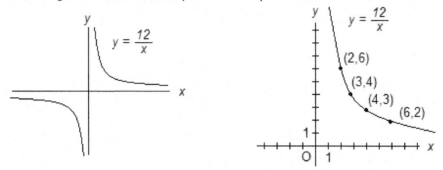

Example: If y varies inversely as x and $y = 8$ when $x = 3$, then what is y when $x = 6$?

Solution 1: Since y varies inversely as x, $y = \frac{k}{x}$ for some constant k. We are given that $y = 8$ when $x = 3$, so that $8 = \frac{k}{3}$, or $k = 24$. Therefore $y = \frac{24}{x}$. When $x = 6$, we have $y = \frac{24}{6} = \mathbf{4}$.

Solution 2: Since y varies inversely as x, xy is a constant. So we get the following equation: $(3)(8) = 6y$ So $24 = 6y$, and $y = \frac{24}{6} = \mathbf{4}$.

* Solution 3: $\frac{(8)(3)}{6} = \mathbf{4}$.

Download additional solutions for free here:

www.thesatmathprep.com/28Les500.html

LESSON 4
STATISTICS

Change Averages to Sums

A problem involving averages often becomes much easier when we first convert the averages to sums. We can easily change an average to a sum using the following simple formula.

Sum = Average · Number

Many problems with averages involve one or more conversions to sums, followed by a subtraction.

Note: The above formula comes from eliminating the denominator in the definition of average.

$$\text{Average} = \frac{\text{Sum}}{\text{Number}}$$

Try to answer the following question using this strategy. **Do not** check the solution until you have attempted this question yourself.

LEVEL 1: STATISTICS

1. The average (arithmetic mean) of three numbers is 50. If two of the numbers are 40 and 65, what is the third number?

   (A) 35
   (B) 40
   (C) 45
   (D) 50

* In this case we are averaging 3 numbers. Thus, the **Number** is 3. The **Average** is given to be 50. So the **Sum** of the 3 numbers is $50 \cdot 3 = 150$. Since we know that two of the numbers are 40 and 65, the third number is $150 - 40 - 65 = 45$, choice (C).

Before we go on, try to solve this problem in two other ways.

(1) By "Starting with Choice (C)."
(2) Algebraically (the way you would do it in school).

43

Solution by starting with choice (C): Let's start with choice (C) and guess that the third number is 45. Then the average of the three numbers is $\frac{40+65+45}{3} = \frac{150}{3} = 50$. Since this is correct, the answer is choice (C).

Algebraic solution: Note that I strongly recommend that you **do not** use this method on the actual SAT!

If we name the third number x, we have

$$\frac{40 + 65 + x}{3} = 50$$
$$105 + x = 150$$
$$x = 45.$$

So the answer is choice (C).

Now try to solve each of the following problems by using the strategy you just learned. The answers to these problems, followed by full solutions are at the end of this lesson. **Do not** look at the answers until you have attempted these problems yourself. Please remember to mark off any problems you get wrong.

LEVEL 1: STATISTICS

2. The average (arithmetic mean) of seven numbers is 100. If the sum of six of the numbers is 646, what is the seventh number?

3. For which of the following lists of 5 numbers is the average (arithmetic mean) less than the median?

   (A) 1, 1, 3, 4, 4
   (B) 1, 2, 3, 5, 6
   (C) 1, 1, 3, 5, 5
   (D) 1, 2, 3, 4, 5

LEVEL 2: STATISTICS

4. The average (arithmetic mean) of three numbers is 114. If one of the numbers is 32, what is the sum of the other two?

5. The average (arithmetic mean) of 22, 50, and y is 50. What is the value of y ?

6. The average (arithmetic mean) of eight numbers is 130. If a ninth number, 40, is added to the group, what is the average of the nine numbers?

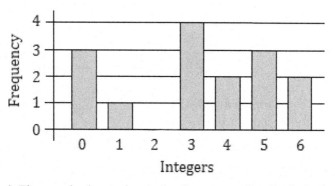

7. * The graph above shows the frequency distribution of a list of randomly generated integers between 0 and 6. What is the mean of the list of numbers?

LEVEL 3: STATISTICS

8. The average (arithmetic mean) of seven numbers is 20. When an eighth number is added, the average of the eight numbers is also 20. What is the eighth number?

Definitions Used in This Lesson

The **average (arithmetic mean)** of a set of numbers is the sum of the numbers in the set divided by the quantity of the numbers in the set.

$$\textbf{Average} = \frac{\textbf{Sum}}{\textbf{Number}}$$

In SAT problems we often use the formula in the following form:

Sum = Average · Number

The **median** of a set of numbers is the middle number when the numbers are arranged in increasing order. If the total number of values in the set is even, then the median is the average of the two middle values.

Answers

1. C   5. 78
2. 54   6. 120
3. A   7. 16/5 or 3.2
4. 310   8. 20

Full Solutions

2.

* Solution by changing averages to sums: We change the average to a sum using the formula

Sum = Average · Number

Here we are averaging 7 numbers. Thus, the **Number** is 7. The **Average** is given to be 100. So the **Sum** of the 7 numbers is $100 \cdot 7 = 700$. Since we know that the sum of six of the numbers is 646, the seventh number is

$$700 - 646 = \mathbf{54}.$$

3.

Solution by changing averages to sums: All of these lists have a median of 3 (this is the number in the middle when the numbers are written in increasing order).

We want the **Average** to be less than 3. So using the formula

Sum = Average · Number

we see that we want the **Sum** to be less than $3 \cdot 5 = 15$.

Let's start with choice (C). The sum is $1 + 1 + 3 + 5 + 5 = 15$.

Let's try (D) next. $1 + 2 + 3 + 4 + 5 = 15$

Let's try (B). $1 + 2 + 3 + 5 + 6 = 17$

Let's try (A). $1 + 1 + 3 + 4 + 4 = 13$

Since 13 is less than 15, the answer is choice (A).

* Quick Solution: With a little experience it is not hard to see that (A) is the answer. Just look at how the numbers are "balanced" about the middle number 3. 1 is two units to the left, and 4 is only 1 unit to the right. You should still compute the sum as a check to verify that the answer is correct.

4.

* Solution by changing averages to sums: We are averaging 3 numbers so that the **Number** is 3. The **Average** is given to be 114. Therefore the **Sum** of the 3 numbers is $114 \cdot 3 = 342$. Since one of the numbers is 32, it follows that the sum of the other two is $342 - 32 = \mathbf{310}$.

Complete algebraic solution: This method is **not** recommended for use on the SAT, but it is included for completeness.

Let x, y, and 32 be the three numbers. We have that $\frac{x+y+32}{3} = 114$. Multiplying each side of this equation by 3 yields $x + y + 32 = 342$. Finally, subtract 32 from each side to get $x + y = \mathbf{310}$.

5.

Solution by changing averages to sums: We are averaging 3 numbers so that the **Number** is 3. The **Average** is given to be 50. Thus, the **Sum** of the 3 numbers is $50 \cdot 3 = 150$. Since we know that two of the numbers are 22 and 50, the third number is $y = 150 - 22 - 50 = \mathbf{78}$.

* Quick solution: Since the average is 50, y must be at the same distance from 50 as 22. The distance between 22 and 50 is $50 - 22 = 28$. It follows that $y = 50 + 28 = \mathbf{78}$.

6.

* Solution by changing averages to sums: At first we are averaging eight numbers. Thus, the **Number** is 8. The **Average** is given to be 130. It follows that the **Sum** of the eight numbers is $130 \cdot 8 = 1040$.

When we add 40 to the group the **Sum** becomes $1040 + 40 = 1080$. Thus, the **Average** of the nine numbers is $\frac{1080}{9} = \mathbf{120}$.

7.

$* \dfrac{3 \cdot 0 + 1 \cdot 1 + 0 \cdot 2 + 4 \cdot 3 + 2 \cdot 4 + 3 \cdot 5 + 2 \cdot 6}{3 + 1 + 4 + 2 + 3 + 2} = \dfrac{1 + 12 + 8 + 15 + 12}{15} = \dfrac{48}{15} = \mathbf{3.2}.$

Notes: (1) According to the graph, 0 occurs 3 times, 1 occurs 1 time, 2 occurs 0 times, 3 occurs 4 times, 4 occurs 2 times, 5 occurs 3 times, and 6 occurs 2 times.

(2) A complete list of the data is

0, 0, 0, 1, 3, 3, 3, 3, 4, 4, 5, 5, 5, 6, 6

(3) Average $= \frac{\text{Sum}}{\text{Number}}$. In other words to compute an average, we add up all the data, and then divide by the number of data points.

8.

* **Solution by changing averages to sums:** The sum of the seven numbers is $20 \cdot 7 = 140$.

The sum of the eight numbers is $20 \cdot 8 = 160$.

The eighth number is $160 - 140 = \mathbf{20}$.

* **Quick solution:** If a list of numbers has an average of 20, then adding the number 20 does not change the average. So the answer is **20**.

See the Challenge Problem in the Optional Material at the end of Lesson 16 for a rigorous treatment of this last explanation.

OPTIONAL MATERIAL

The following questions will test your understanding of the definitions used in this lesson. These are **not** SAT questions.

Compute the average (arithmetic mean) and median of the following lists of numbers.

1. $1, 2, 3, 4, 5$
2. $3, 3, 3, 3, 3$
3. $5, 3, 1, -1, -3, -5$
4. $21, 57, 32, 48, 1, 101$
5. $1, 2, 3, 4, 5,..., 99$
6. x, y, z, where $x < y < z$
7. $1, 2, 5, 6, 10, 14, 15, 18, 19$

Answers

1. average = median = 3
2. average = median = 3
3. average = median = 0
4. average = $43\frac{1}{3} = \frac{130}{3} \approx 43.3$, median = 40
5. average = median = 50
6. average = $\frac{x+y+z}{3}$, median = y
7. average = median = 10

Tips for Computing These Quickly

You can (and should) compute each of these directly. But in addition you should try to get the answers quickly using some shortcuts.

1. In a list of consecutive integers, the average (arithmetic mean) and median are equal.

2. If all the numbers in a list are the same, the average and median are equal to that number.

3. **Method 1:** Notice how all of the numbers are "balanced" about 0.

Method 2: Note that the sum is 0 (a quick way to see this is by observing that for each positive number the corresponding negative number is there also).

5. In a list of consecutive integers, the average (arithmetic mean) and median are equal to the average of the first and last number:

$$\frac{1+99}{2} = \frac{100}{2} = 50.$$

7. Notice how all of the numbers are "balanced" about 10 (for example, the distance from 6 to 10 is the same as the distance from 14 to 10).

Download additional solutions for free here:

www.thesatmathprep.com/28Les500.html

LESSON 5
HEART OF ALGEBRA

Reminder: Before beginning this lesson remember to redo the problems from Lesson 1 that you have marked off. Do not "unmark" a question unless you get it correct.

Take a guess

Sometimes the answer choices themselves cannot be substituted in for the unknown or unknowns in the problem. But that doesn't mean you can't guess your own numbers. Try to make as reasonable a guess as possible, but don't over think it. Keep trying until you zero in on the correct value.

Try to answer the following question using this strategy. **Do not** check the solution until you have attempted this question yourself.

LEVEL 3: HEART OF ALGEBRA

1. Bill has cows, pigs and chickens on his farm. The number of chickens he has is three times the number of pigs, and the number of pigs he has is 2 more than the number of cows. Which of the following could be the total number of these animals?

   (A) 15
   (B) 16
   (C) 17
   (D) 18

* Solution by taking a guess: Let's take a guess and say that Bill has 3 cows. Then he has $3 + 2 = 5$ pigs, and $3 \cdot 5 = 15$ chickens. It follows that the total number of animals is $3 + 5 + 15 = 23$. This is too big. So let's guess that Bill has less cows, say 1. Then he has $1 + 2 = 3$ pigs, and $3 \cdot 3 = 9$ chickens. The total number of animals is then $1 + 3 + 9 = 13$. This is too small. So Bill must have 2 cows, $2 + 2 = 4$ pigs, and $3 \cdot 4 = 12$ chickens. Therefore the total is $2 + 4 + 12 = 18$ animals. Thus, the answer is choice (D).

50

Note: We were pretty unlucky to have to take 3 guesses before getting the answer, but even so, not too much time was used.

Before we go on, try to solve this problem the way you might do it in school.

Please note: I am **not** recommending that you solve the problem this way on the SAT. It is good to go through the algebraic solution at home however to get a better mathematical understanding of the problem and to observe potential traps that you could fall into.

Algebraic solution: If we let x represent the number of cows, then the number of pigs is $x + 2$, and the number of chickens is $3(x + 2)$. Thus, the total number of animals is

$$x + (x + 2) + 3(x + 2) = x + x + 2 + 3x + 6 = 5x + 8.$$

So some possible totals are 13, 18, 23, ... which we get by substituting 1, 2, 3, ... for x. Substituting 2 in for x gives 18 which is answer choice (D).

Warning: Many students incorrectly interpret "three times the number of pigs" as $3x + 2$. This is incorrect. The number of pigs is $x + 2$, and so "three times the number of pigs" is $3(x + 2) = 3x + 6$.

You're doing great! Let's practice a bit more. Try to solve each of the following problems by taking a guess. Then, if possible, solve each problem another way. The answers to these problems, followed by full solutions are at the end of this lesson. **Do not** look at the answers until you have attempted these problems yourself. Please remember to mark off any problems you get wrong.

LEVEL 1: HEART OF ALGEBRA

2. If $3y - 18 = 15$, then $y - 6 =$

   (A) 5
   (B) 10
   (C) 15
   (D) 20

3. If $4x - 12 = 8$, then $42 - 3x =$

4. If $6y - 30 = 42$, then $y - 5 =$

5.   If $k > 0$, for what value of k will $k^2 - 4 = 32$?

LEVEL 2: HEART OF ALGEBRA

$$\sqrt{10b^2 - 9} + x = 0$$

6.   If $b > 0$ and $x = -9$ in the equation above, what is the value of b?

LEVEL 3: HEART OF ALGEBRA

7.   What is one possible value of x for which $x < 6 < \frac{1}{x}$?

8.   If $3^x = 11$, then $3^{2x} =$

   (A) 5.5
   (B) 22
   (C) 33
   (D) 121

Answers

1. D   5. 6
2. A   6. 3
3. 27   7. $0 < x < .167$
4. 7   8. D

Note: The full solution for question 4 has been omitted because its solution is very similar to the solution to question 2.

Full Solutions

   2.

Solution by taking a guess: Let's start with a "random" guess for y, say $y = 10$. So let's plug 10 in for y in the first equation.

$$3y - 18 = 15$$
$$3 \cdot 10 - 18 = 15$$
$$30 - 18 = 15$$
$$12 = 15$$

It looks as though 10 is a little too small. $y = 11$ should do the trick.

$$3y - 18 = 15$$
$$3 \cdot 11 - 18 = 15$$
$$33 - 18 = 15$$
$$15 = 15$$

So y is, in fact, 11. Thus, $y - 6 = 11 - 6 = 5$, and the answer is (A).

Algebraic solution: We solve for y algebraically.

$$3y - 18 = 15$$
$$3y = 33$$
$$y = 11$$

So $y - 6 = 11 - 6 = 5$, and the answer is choice (A).

* Quicker algebraic solution: We solve for $y - 6$ algebraically.

$$3y - 18 = 15$$
$$3(y - 6) = 15$$
$$y - 6 = 5$$

Thus, the answer is choice (A).

    3.

Solution by taking a guess: Let's start with a "random" guess for x, let's say $x = 6$. So let's plug 6 in for x in the first equation.

$$4x - 12 = 8$$
$$4 \cdot 6 - 12 = 8$$
$$24 - 12 = 8$$
$$12 = 8$$

Our guess was too big. So let's take a smaller guess like 5.

$$4x - 12 = 8$$
$$4 \cdot 5 - 12 = 8$$
$$20 - 12 = 8$$
$$8 = 8$$

It worked. So x is 5. Thus $42 - 3x = 42 - 3 \cdot 5 = 42 - 15 = \mathbf{27}$.

* Algebraic solution: We solve the first equation for x to get $x = 5$. Then $42 - 3x = 42 - 3 \cdot 5 = 42 - 15 = \mathbf{27}$.

5.

* Solution by taking a guess: Let's take a guess for k, say $k = 5$. Then $k^2 - 4 = 5^2 - 4 = 25 - 4 = 21$. This is too small. So let's try a larger value for k, say $k = 6$. Then $k^2 - 4 = 6^2 - 4 = 36 - 4 = 32$. Thus, the answer is **6**.

Algebraic solution:

$$k^2 - 4 = 32$$
$$k^2 = 36$$
$$k = 6$$

Remark: The equation $k^2 = 36$ has two solutions: $k = 6$ and $k = -6$. In this question we are given that $k > 0$, so we reject the negative solution. In easy problems (Level 1 and Level 2), it is pretty safe to reject the negative solution (or not even think about it), but in medium and hard problems (Levels 3, 4 and 5) you may need to be more careful.

* Mental math: $36 - 4 = 32$. So $k = 6$.

Remark: For more information on this technique see the optional material at the end of Lesson 1.

6.

Solution by taking a guess: When we replace x by -9 we get

$$\sqrt{10b^2 - 9} - 9 = 0.$$

Let's start with a "random" guess for b, let's say $b = 5$. So let's plug 5 in for b in the equation above.

$$\sqrt{10(5)^2 - 9} - 9 = \sqrt{10 \cdot 25 - 9} - 9 = \sqrt{250 - 9} - 9 = \sqrt{241} - 9.$$

Since $\sqrt{241} > 9$, our guess was too big.

Let's try $b = 3$ next. We then have the following.

$$\sqrt{10(3)^2 - 9} - 9 = \sqrt{90 - 9} - 9 = \sqrt{81} - 9 = 9 - 9 = 0.$$

So the answer is **3**.

Algebraic solution: As in the previous solution we replace x by -9 to get

$$\sqrt{10b^2 - 9} - 9 = 0, \text{ or equivalently, } \sqrt{10b^2 - 9} = 9$$

We square each side of this last equation to get $10b^2 - 9 = 81$.

We then add 9 to get $10b^2 = 90$, divide by 10 to get $b^2 = 9$. Since $3^2 = 9$, the answer is **3**.

Remark: To solve the equation $b^2 = 9$ formally requires the **square root property**. There are two solutions to this equation: $b = 3$ and $b = -3$. See Lesson 19 for more on the square root property.

7.

* Solution by taking a guess: Let's try to guess what x is. Here are some guesses using our calculator to get $\frac{1}{x}$ as a decimal.

x	$1/x$
4	.25
2	.5
1	1
.5	2
.1	10

We see that $.1 < 6 < 10$. So we can grid in **.1**.

Choosing Guesses: If guesses of a certain kind aren't working, try a number of a different kind. For example, in this problem positive integers weren't working, so we switched to decimals less than 1. In general, trying extreme cases is always good. In this case a large integer and a small decimal would get the answer quickly. In other examples, extreme cases might consist of a positive integer, a negative integer, a positive fraction and a negative fraction. Note that attempting negative numbers would be a waste of time in this problem since we cannot grid in a negative number.

Algebraic solution: If $6 < \frac{1}{x}$, then we have $\frac{1}{6} > x$, or equivalently, $x < \frac{1}{6}$, or as a decimal $x < .166666...$ So we can grid in any answer strictly between 0 and .167. Note that an answer of .167 will be marked wrong (and 0 will be marked wrong as well).

8.

Solution by taking a guess: Let's try to guess what x is. $3^2 = 9$, and $3^3 = 27$. So x is between 2 and 3. Now, $3^{2\cdot2} = 3^4 = 81$ and $3^{2\cdot3} = 3^6 = 729$. Therefore the answer is between 81 and 729. Thus, the answer must be choice (D).

* Algebraic solution: $3^{2x} = (3^x)^2 = 11^2 = 121$. Thus, the answer is choice (D).

See the optional material below for a review of the basic laws of exponents.

OPTIONAL MATERIAL

Basic Laws of Exponents

Here is a brief review of the basic laws of exponents.

Law	Example
$x^0 = 1$	$3^0 = 1$
$x^1 = x$	$9^1 = 9$
$x^a x^b = x^{a+b}$	$x^3 x^5 = x^8$
$x^a / x^b = x^{a-b}$	$x^{11}/x^4 = x^7$
$(x^a)^b = x^{ab}$	$(x^5)^3 = x^{15}$
$(xy)^a = x^a y^a$	$(xy)^4 = x^4 y^4$
$(x/y)^a = x^a/y^a$	$(x/y)^6 = x^6/y^6$

Now let's practice. Simplify the following expressions using the basic laws of exponents.

1. $5^2 \cdot 5^3$

2. $\dfrac{5^3}{5^2}$

3. $\dfrac{x^5 \cdot x^3}{x^8}$

4. $(2^3)^4$

5. $\dfrac{(xy)^7 (yz)^2}{y^9}$

6. $\left(\dfrac{2}{3}\right)^3 \left(\dfrac{9}{4}\right)^2$

7. $\dfrac{x^4 + x^2}{x^2}$

8. $\dfrac{(x^{10}+x^9+x^8)(y^5+y^4)}{y^4(x^2+x+1)}$

Answers

1. $5^5 = 3125$

2. $5^1 = 5$

3. $\dfrac{x^8}{x^8} = 1$

4. $2^{12} = 4096$

5. $\dfrac{x^7 y^7 y^2 z^2}{y^9} = \dfrac{x^7 y^9 z^2}{y^9} = x^7 z^2$

6. $\dfrac{2^3}{3^3} \cdot \dfrac{9^2}{4^2} = \dfrac{2^3}{3^3} \cdot \dfrac{(3^2)^2}{(2^2)^2} = \dfrac{2^3}{3^3} \cdot \dfrac{3^4}{2^4} = \dfrac{3^1}{2^1} = \dfrac{3}{2}$

7. $\dfrac{x^2(x^2+1)}{x^2} = x^2 + 1$

8. $\dfrac{x^8(x^2+x+1)y^4(y+1)}{y^4(x^2+x+1)} = x^8(y+1)$

LESSON 6
GEOMETRY

Reminder: Before beginning this lesson remember to redo the problems from Lesson 2 that you have marked off. Do not "unmark" a question unless you get it correct.

Turn to page 50 and review **Take a guess**. Then try to answer the following question using this strategy. **Do not** check the solution until you have attempted this question yourself.

LEVEL 1: GEOMETRY

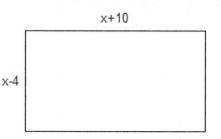

1. If the perimeter of the rectangle above is 56, what is the value of x?

* Solution by taking a guess: Recall that we get the **perimeter** of a rectangle by adding up all four sides. Let's start with $x = 10$ as our first guess. Then $x - 4 = 10 - 4 = 6$ and $x + 10 = 10 + 10 = 20$. So the perimeter is $2(6) + 2(20) = 12 + 40 = 52$, a bit too small. So let's try $x = 11$. Then $x - 4 = 11 - 4 = 7$ and $x + 10 = 11 + 10 = 21$. So the perimeter is $2(7) + 2(21) = 14 + 42 = 56$. This is correct so that the answer is **11**.

Before we go on, try to solve this problem algebraically.

Algebraic solution:

$$P = 2l + 2w$$
$$56 = 2(x + 10) + 2(x - 4)$$
$$56 = 2x + 20 + 2x - 8$$
$$56 = 4x + 12$$
$$44 = 4x$$
$$11 = x$$

So the answer is **11**.

You're doing great! Let's just practice a bit more. Try to solve each of the following problems by using the strategy we just reviewed. Then, if possible, solve each problem another way. The answers to these problems, followed by some full solutions are at the end of this lesson. **Do not** look at the answers until you have attempted these problems yourself. Please remember to mark off any problems you get wrong.

LEVEL 1: GEOMETRY

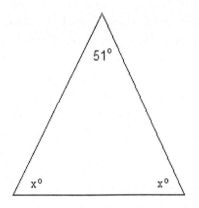

2. In the triangle above, what is the value of x ?

3. If the degree measures of the three angles of a triangle are $k°$, $k°$, and $70°$, what is the value of k?

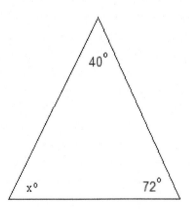

4. In the triangle above, $x=$

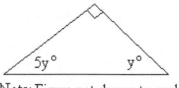

Note: Figure not drawn to scale.

5. In the right triangle above, what is the value of y?

6. What is the radius of a circle whose circumference is 3π?

LEVEL 3: GEOMETRY

7. The volume of a right circular cylinder is 1024π cubic centimeters. If the height is twice the base radius of the cylinder, what is the base radius of the cylinder?

8. A rectangle has a perimeter of 22 meters and an area of 28 square meters. What is the shortest of the side lengths, in meters, of the rectangle?

Definitions and Formulas Used in This Lesson

Definitions of a **triangle**, **quadrilateral**, **rectangle**, **circle**, and **cylinder** can be found on page 29. The formulas used in this lesson can be found on page 29 as well.

Answers

1. 11
2. 64.5
3. 55
4. 68

5. 15
6. 3/2 or 1.5
7. 8
8. 4

Note: Full solutions for several questions have been omitted because their solutions are very similar to the solutions to other questions from this lesson and from Lesson 2.

Full Solutions

2.

Solution by taking a guess: Recall that a triangle has angle measures which sum to 180 degrees. We take a guess for x, let's say that $x = 60$. The sum of the angle measures is $x + x + 51 = 60 + 60 + 51 = 171$ degrees, too small. Let's now try $x = 65$. Then the sum of the angle measures is $x + x + 51 = 65 + 65 + 51 = 181$ degrees, a bit too big. Let's try $x = 64.5$. The angle measures then sum to $x + x + 51 = 64.5 + 64.5 + 51 = 180$ degrees. So the answer is **64.5**.

An algebraic solution: There are 180 degrees in a triangle, so we solve the equation $x + x + 51 = 180$ to get $2x + 51 = 180$, and so $2x = 129$. Finally, $x = \frac{129}{2} = \mathbf{64.5}$.

* Mental math: $180 - 51 = 129$. Divide 129 by 2 to get $x = \mathbf{64.5}$.

6.

Solution by taking a guess: The circumference of a circle is $C = 2\pi r$. Let's start with a guess of say $r = 1$. Then $C = 2\pi r = 2\pi(1) = 2\pi$, too small. It looks like $r = 1.5$ should work. In this case, we have that $C = 2\pi(1.5) = 3\pi$. So the answer is indeed **1.5**.

* Algebraic solution: We use the circumference formula $C = 2\pi r$, and substitute 3π in for C.

$$C = 2\pi r$$
$$3\pi = 2\pi r$$
$$\frac{3\pi}{2\pi} = r$$
$$\frac{3}{2} = r$$

So $r = \mathbf{3/2}$ or $\mathbf{1.5}$.

7.

Solution by taking a guess: Let's start with a guess of $r = 6$. Then $h = 12$, so that $V = \pi r^2 h = \pi(6)^2(12) = 432\pi$, too small. Let's try $r = 8$ next. Then $h = 16$, and so $V = \pi r^2 h = \pi(8)^2(16) = 1024\pi$. This is correct, and so the base radius is **8**.

* Algebraic solution:

$$V = \pi r^2 h$$
$$1024\pi = \pi r^2 (2r)$$
$$512 = r^3$$
$$8 = r.$$

Therefore the answer is **8**.

8.

Solution by taking a guess: Let's guess that the shortest side of the rectangle is 5 meters long. Then the length of the two shorter sides of the rectangle adds up to 10 meters. Since the perimeter is 22, it follows that the longest side must have length $\frac{22-10}{2} = \frac{12}{2} = 6$. So the area is $(5)(6) = 30$. this is too big.

This time let's guess that the shortest side of the rectangle is 4 meters long. Then the length of the two shorter sides of the rectangle adds up to 8 meters. Since the perimeter is 22, it follows that the longest side must have length $\frac{22-8}{2} = \frac{14}{2} = 7$. So the area is $(4)(7) = 28$. this is correct. So the answer is **4**.

Remarks: (1) If one side of the rectangle has a length of 4 meters, then the opposite side also has a length of 4 meters. Since the perimeter is 22 meters, this leaves $22 - 4 - 4 = 14$ meters for the other two sides. It follows that a longer side of the rectangle has length $\frac{14}{2} = 7$ meters.

(2) When guessing the shortest side of the rectangle we can use the area instead of the perimeter to find the shortest side. For example, if we guess that the shortest side is 4, then since the area is 28 it follows that the longest side is 7. We would then check to see if we get the right perimeter. In this case we have $P = 2(4) + 2(7) = 22$ which is correct.

Algebraic solution: We are given that $2x + 2y = 22$ and $xy = 28$. If we divide each side of the first equation by 2, we get $x + y = 11$. Subtracting each side of this equation by x, we get $y = 11 - x$.

We replace y by $11 - x$ in the second equation to get $x(11 - x) = 28$. Distributing the x on the left yields $11x - x^2 = 28$. Subtracting $11x$ and adding x^2 to each side of this equation gives us $0 = x^2 - 11x + 28$. The right hand side can be factored to give $0 = (x - 7)(x - 4)$.

So we have $x - 7 = 0$ or $x - 4 = 0$. So $x = 7$ or $x = 4$. Since the question asks for the shortest of the side lengths, the answer is $x = \mathbf{4}$.

OPTIONAL MATERIAL

The following questions will test your understanding of formulas used in this lesson. These are **not** SAT questions.

1. Find the circumference of a circle with each of the following radii.

$$3 \qquad \pi \qquad x \qquad x^2 + 5$$

2. Find the radius of a circle with each of the following circumferences.

$$2\pi \qquad \pi \qquad 7\pi \qquad 5 \qquad C \qquad x - 2$$

3. Find the volume of a cylinder with each of the following base radii and heights.

$$r = h = 2 \qquad r = 3, h = 4 \qquad r = \pi, h = 2\pi \qquad r = x + 1, h = 2x$$

4. Find the height of a cylinder with volume 2π and base radius 5.

5. Find the base radius of a cylinder with volume 100 and height 10.

Answers

1. 6π, $2\pi^2$, $2\pi x$, $2\pi(x^2 + 5)$

2. $1, \dfrac{1}{2}, \dfrac{7}{2}, \dfrac{5}{2\pi}, \dfrac{C}{2\pi}, \dfrac{x-2}{2\pi}$

3. 8π, 36π, $2\pi^4$, $\pi(x + 1)^2(2x) = 2\pi x(x + 1)^2$

4. $2\pi = \pi(5)^2 h$. So $h = \dfrac{2\pi}{\pi(5)^2} = \dfrac{2}{25}$

5. $100 = \pi r^2(10)$. So $r^2 = \dfrac{100}{10\pi} = \dfrac{10}{\pi}$. So $r = \sqrt{\dfrac{10}{\pi}}$

LESSON 7
PASSPORT TO ADVANCED MATH

Reminder: Before beginning this lesson remember to redo the problems from Lesson 3 that you have marked off. Do not "unmark" a question unless you get it correct.

The Distributive Property

The **distributive property** says that for all real numbers a, b, and c

$$a(b + c) = ab + ac$$

More specifically, this property says that the operation of multiplication distributes over addition. The distributive property is very important as it allows us to multiply and factor algebraic expressions.

Numeric example: Show that $2(3 + 4) = 2 \cdot 3 + 2 \cdot 4$

Solution: $2(3 + 4) = 2 \cdot 7 = 14$ and $2 \cdot 3 + 2 \cdot 4 = 6 + 8 = 14$.

Geometric Justification: The following picture gives a physical representation of the distributive property for this example.

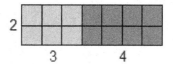

Note that the area of the light grey rectangle is $2 \cdot 3$, the area of the dark grey rectangle is $2 \cdot 4$, and the area of the whole rectangle is $2(3 + 4)$.

Algebraic examples: Use the distributive property to write each algebraic expression in an equivalent form.

(1) $2(x + 1)$ 　　　　(2) $x(y - 3)$ 　　　　(3) $-(x - y)$

Solutions: (1) $2(x + 1) = 2x + 2$

(2) $x(y - 3) = xy - 3x$

(3) $-(x - y) = -x + y$

Try this SAT math problem where the distributive property can be used.

63

LEVEL 1: ADVANCED MATH

$$5x(2y + z)$$

1. Which of the following is equivalent to the expression above?

    (A) $7xy + 5z$
    (B) $7xy + 5xz$
    (C) $10xy + xz$
    (D) $10xy + 5xz$

* Solution using the distributive property:

$$5x(2y + z) = 5x \cdot 2y + 5x \cdot z = 10xy + 5xz$$

So the answer is choice (D).

Notes: (1) $5x \cdot 2y = 5 \cdot 2 \cdot x \cdot y = 10xy$. Similarly, $5x \cdot z = 5xz$.

(2) This problem can also be solved by using the strategy of picking numbers. You will learn this strategy in Lesson 9. In fact, many of the problems in this section can be solved by picking numbers. The methods presented in this lesson however will generally be much faster.

Factoring

When we use the distributive property in the opposite direction, we usually call it **factoring**.

Examples: (1) $2x + 4y = 2(x + 2y)$

(2) $3x + 5xy = x(3 + 5y)$

(3) $6xy + 9yz = 3y(2x + 3z)$

Try this SAT math problem that can be solved by factoring.

LEVEL 1: ADVANCED MATH

2. If $10xz - 15yz = az(2x - by)$ where a and b are positive real numbers, what is the value of $a + b$?

* Solution by factoring:

$$10xz - 15yz = 5z(2x - 3y)$$

So $a = 5, b = 3$, and therefore $a + b = 5 + 3 = $ **8**.

Addition and Subtraction of Polynomials

We add polynomials by simply combining like terms. We can change any subtraction problem to an addition problem by first distributing the minus sign. Let's look at an example.

LEVEL 2: ADVANCED MATH

$$(-3x^2y + 2xy^2) - (-3x^2y - 2xy^2)$$

3. Which of the following is equivalent to the expression above?

(A) 0
(B) $-6x^2y$
(C) $4xy^2$
(D) $-6x^2y + 4xy^2$

* Algebraic solution:

$$(-3x^2y + 2xy^2) - (-3x^2y - 2xy^2)$$
$$= -3x^2y + 2xy^2 + 3x^2y + 2xy^2$$
$$= (-3x^2y + 3x^2y) + (2xy^2 + 2xy^2) = 0 + 4xy^2 = 4xy^2$$

This is choice (C).

Multiplication of Polynomials

Most students are familiar with the mnemonic FOIL to help them multiply two binomials (polynomials with 2 terms) together. As a simple example, we have

$$(x + 1)(x - 2) = x^2 - 2x + x - 2 = x^2 - x - 2$$

Unfortunately this method works ONLY for binomials. It does not extend to polynomials with more than 2 terms. Let's demonstrate another way to multiply polynomials with the same example.

We begin by lining up the polynomials vertically:

$$\begin{array}{r} x + 1 \\ \underline{x - 2} \end{array}$$

We multiply the -2 on the bottom by each term on top, moving from right to left. First note that -2 times 1 is -2:

$$\begin{array}{r} x + 1 \\ \underline{x - 2} \\ -2 \end{array}$$

65

Next note that -2 times x is $-2x$:

$$\begin{array}{r} x + 1 \\ \underline{x - 2} \\ -2x - 2 \end{array}$$

Now we multiply the x on the bottom by each term on top, moving from right to left. This time as we write the answers we leave one blank space on the right:

$$\begin{array}{r} x + 1 \\ \underline{x - 2} \\ -2x - 2 \\ \underline{x^2 + x } \end{array}$$

Finally, we add:

$$\begin{array}{r} x + 1 \\ \underline{x - 2} \\ -2x - 2 \\ \underline{x^2 + x } \\ x^2 - x - 2 \end{array}$$

Try to use this algorithm to solve the following problem.

LEVEL 2: ADVANCED MATH

4. The expression $(3b - 2)(b + 5)$ is equivalent to:

(A) $3b^2 - 7$
(B) $3b^2 - 10$
(C) $3b^2 - 2b - 7$
(D) $3b^2 + 13b - 10$

* Algebraic solution:

$$\begin{array}{r} 3b - 2 \\ \underline{b + 5} \\ 15b - 10 \\ \underline{3b^2 - 2b } \\ 3b^2 + 13b - 10 \end{array}$$

This is choice (D).

You're doing great! Let's just practice a bit more. Try to solve each of the following problems by using one of the techniques you just learned. The answers to these problems, followed by full solutions are at the end of this lesson. **Do not** look at the answers until you have attempted these problems yourself. Please remember to mark off any problems you get wrong.

Level 2: Advanced Math

5. What is the value of $d - 2$ if $(6d - 3) - (2 - d) = 9$?

$$5(3x - 2)(2x + 1)$$

6. Which of the following is equivalent to the expression above?

(A) $30x^2 - 10$
(B) $30x^2 - 5x - 10$
(C) $25x^2 - 20$
(D) $15x$

Level 3: Advanced Math

7. What polynomial must be added to $x^2 + 3x - 5$ so that the sum is $5x^2 - 8$?

(A) $4x^2 - 5x + 6$
(B) $4x^2 - 3x - 3$
(C) $5x^2 - 3x - 3$
(D) $5x^2 + 3x + 6$

8. For all x, $(x^2 - 3x + 1)(x + 2) = ?$

(A) $x^3 - x^2 - 5x + 2$
(B) $x^3 - x^2 - 5x - 2$
(C) $x^3 - x^2 + 5x + 2$
(D) $x^3 + x^2 - 5x + 2$

Definitions Used in This Lesson

A **polynomial in** x has the form $a_n x^n + a_{n-1} x^{n-1} + \cdots + a_1 x + a_0$ where $a_0, a_1, \ldots, a_n$ are real numbers. **Ex:** $x^2 + 2x - 35$ is a polynomial.

Answers

1. D	5. 0
2. 8	6. B
3. C	7. B
4. D	8. A

Full Solutions

5.

* Solution using the distributive property:

$$(6d - 3) - (2 - d) = 6d - 3 - 2 + d = 7d - 5$$

So the given equation is equivalent to $7d - 5 = 9$. We add 5 to each side of this last equation to get $7d = 9 + 5 = 14$. We then divide by 7 to get $d = \frac{14}{7} = 2$. So $d - 2 = 2 - 2 = \mathbf{0}$.

6.

$$* \, 5(3x - 2)(2x + 1) = 5(6x^2 + 3x - 4x - 2) = 5(6x^2 - x - 2)$$
$$= 30x^2 - 5x - 10$$

This is choice (B).

Note: We can multiply $(3x - 2)$ and $(2x + 1)$ either by using FOIL or by using the algorithm given in this lesson.

7.

* Algebraic solution: We need to subtract $(5x^2 - 8) - (x^2 + 3x - 5)$. We first eliminate the parentheses by distributing the minus sign:

$$5x^2 - 8 - x^2 - 3x + 5$$

Finally, we combine like terms to get $4x^2 - 3x - 3$, choice (B).

Remark: Pay careful attention to the minus and plus signs in the solution above. In particular, make sure you are distributing correctly.

8.

* Algebraic solution: We multiply the two polynomials.

$$
\begin{array}{r}
x^2 - 3x + 1 \\
x + 2 \\
\hline
2x^2 - 6x + 2 \\
x^3 - 3x^2 + x + 0 \\
\hline
x^3 - x^2 - 5x + 2
\end{array}
$$

This is choice (A).

LESSON 8
PROBLEM SOLVING

Reminder: Before beginning this lesson remember to redo the problems from Lesson 4 that you have marked off. Do not "unmark" a question unless you get it correct.

Simple Probability Principle

To compute a simple probability where all outcomes are equally likely, divide the number of "successes" by the total number of outcomes.

Try to answer the following question using the simple probability principle. **Do not** check the solution until you have attempted this question yourself.

LEVEL 2: PROBLEM SOLVING

3, 5, 6, 15, 27, 35, 45, 75

1. A number is to be selected at random from the list above. What is the probability that the number selected will be a multiple of both 3 and 5?

* The total number of outcomes is 8. The number of "successes" is 3. Therefore the probability is **3/8** or **.375**.

Notes: (1) In this problem a "success" is a number that is a multiple of both 3 and 5.

(2) You can check if each number is a "success" by dividing the number by 3 and by 5. If you get an integer in both cases, then the number is a "success." Otherwise it is not. For example, $27/3 = 9$ and $27/5 = 5.4$. Since 5.4 is not an integer, the number 27 is <u>not</u> a "success."

(3) You can check if each number is a "success" more quickly by dividing the number by 15. If you get an integer, then the number is a "success." Otherwise it is not. For example, $27/15 = 1.8$ which is not an integer. Therefore the number 27 is <u>not</u> a "success."

(4) The "successes" are 15, 45, and 75.

Conditional Probability

A **conditional probability** measures the probability of an event given that another event has occurred. Let's use an example to illustrate conditional probability.

LEVEL 2: PROBLEM SOLVING

Questions 2 - 3 refer to the following information.

A survey was conducted among a randomly chosen sample of 100 males and 100 females to gather data on family size. The data are shown in the table below.

	Have siblings	Do not have siblings	Total
Men	75	25	100
Women	63	37	100
Total	138	62	200

2. According to the table, what is the probability that a randomly selected man does not have siblings?

* There are a total of 100 men, and of these men 25 do not have siblings. So the desired probability is $\frac{25}{100} = \mathbf{1/4}$ or $\mathbf{.25}$.

Notes: (1) The denominator of the fraction is 100, the total number of men. To find this number we look in the column labeled "Total" and the row labeled "Men."

(2) The numerator of the fraction is 25, the number of men who do not have siblings. To find this number we look in the column labeled "Do not have siblings" and the row labeled "Men."

Technical Remarks: (1) In this question we are being asked to use the table to compute a conditional probability. Let's name the events as follows: M will stand for "the person selected is a man," and $\sim S$ will stand for "the person selected does not have siblings" (we are using the symbol $\sim$ here for the word "not").

(2) The requested probability is $P(\sim S|M)$. This is read as "the probability that the person selected does not have siblings given that the person selected is a man" (in particular, the vertical line is read "given"). We can say this more simply as "the probability that a selected man does not have siblings."

(3) For the total, we use the Total column and the "Men" row. So the total is 100.

For the successes we use the "Does not have siblings" column and the "Men" row. This is 25

3. * According to the table, what is the probability that a randomly selected person with siblings is female?

* There are 138 people who do have siblings, and of these 63 are women. So the desired probability is $\frac{63}{138} \approx .4565217$. So we can grid in .**456** or .**457**.

Now try to solve each of the following problems. The answers to these problems, followed by full solutions are at the end of this lesson. **Do not** look at the answers until you have attempted these problems yourself. Please remember to mark off any problems you get wrong.

LEVEL 3: PROBLEM SOLVING

Questions 4 - 7 refer to the following information.

The data in the table below categorizes the GPAs of the students from two high schools.

	Less than 2.5	Between 2.5 and 3.5	Greater than 3.5	Total
School A	272	117	36	425
School B	146	308	121	575
Total	358	425	217	1000

4. * If a student with a GPA between 2.5 and 3.5 is chosen at random, what is the probability that the student goes to school B?

71

5.   * What is the probability that a randomly selected student is from school A with a GPA greater than 3.5?

6.   * If a student from School A is chosen at random, what is the probability that the student has a GPA of at least 2.5?

Questions 7 - 8 refer to the following information.

A survey was conducted among a randomly chosen sample of 250 single men and 250 single women about whether they owned any dogs or cats. The table below displays a summary of the survey results.

	Dogs Only	Cats Only	Both	Neither	Total
Men	92	14	18	126	250
Women	75	42	35	98	250
Total	167	56	53	224	500

7.   * According to the table, what is the probability that a randomly selected woman is a dog owner?

8.   * According to the table, what is the probability that a randomly selected person with no pets is a man?

Answers

1. 3/8 or .375   5. .036
2. 1/4 or .25   6. 9/25 or .36
3. .456 or .457   7. .44
4. .724 or .725   8. 9/16, .562 or .563

Full Solutions

4.

* This is a conditional probability. We want the probability the student goes to school B *given* the student has a GPA between 2.5 and 3.5. This is $\frac{308}{425} \approx .724$ or $.725$.

5.

* There are 36 students from school A with a GPA greater than 3.5, and there are a total of 1000 students. So the desired probability is $\frac{36}{1000} = .036$.

6.

* This is a conditional probability. We want the probability the student has a GPA of at least 2.5 *given* the student is from school A. Note that a student has a GPA of at least 2.5 if the student has a GPA between 2.5 and 3.5 **or** the student has a GPA greater than 3.5. So the desired probability is $\frac{117+36}{425} = 9/25$ or $.36$.

7.

* There are a total of 250 women, and of these women $75 + 35 = 110$ own dogs. So the desired probability is $\frac{110}{250} = .44$.

Notes: (1) There are two columns that represent people who said they own dogs: the column labeled "Dogs Only," and the column labeled "Both."

Remember that the word "Both" indicates both dog and cat ownership, and in particular dog ownership.

(2) The denominator of the fraction is 250, the total number of women.

(3) The numerator of the fraction is the number of women who said they own dogs. There are 75 women who said they own dogs only, and 35 women who said they own both dogs and cats. Therefore there are a total of $75 + 35 = 110$ women who said they own dogs.

Technical Remarks: (1) In this question we are being asked to use the table to compute a conditional probability. Let's name the events as follows: W will stand for "the person selected is a woman," D will stand for "the person owns dogs only," and B will stand for "the person selected owns both cats and dogs."

(2) The event $D \cup B$ stands for "the person selected owns dogs only *or* the person selected owns both cats and dogs." This can be stated more simply as "the person selected is a dog owner."

(3) The requested probability is $P(D \cup B|W)$. This is read as "the probability that the person selected is a dog owner given that the person selected is a woman" (in particular, the vertical line is read "given"). We can say this more simply as "the probability that a selected woman is a dog owner."

(4) For the total, we use the total column in the "Women" row. So the total is 250.

For the successes we use the "Dogs Only" and "Both" columns and the "Women" row. This is $75 + 35 = 110$.

    8.

* There are 224 people who said they own no pets, and of these 126 are men. So the desired probability is $\frac{126}{224} = \mathbf{9/16}$.

Note: We can also grid in $.562$ or $.563$.

Download additional solutions for free here:

www.thesatmathprep.com/28Les500.html

LESSON 9
HEART OF ALGEBRA

Reminder: Before beginning this lesson remember to redo the problems from Lessons 1 and 5 that you have marked off. Do not "unmark" a question unless you get it correct.

Pick a Number

A problem may become much easier to understand and to solve by substituting a specific number in for a variable. Just make sure that you choose a number that satisfies the given conditions.

Here are some guidelines when picking numbers.

(1) Pick a number that is simple but not too simple. In general you might want to avoid picking 0 or 1 (but 2 is usually a good choice).

(2) Try to avoid picking numbers that appear in the problem.

(3) When picking two or more numbers try to make them all different.

(4) Most of the time picking numbers only allows you to eliminate answer choices. So do not just choose the first answer choice that comes out to the correct answer. If multiple answers come out correct you need to pick a new number and start again. But you only have to check the answer choices that have not yet been eliminated.

(5) If there are fractions in the question a good choice might be the least common denominator (lcd) or a multiple of the lcd.

(6) In percent problems choose the number 100.

(7) Do not pick a negative number as a possible answer to a grid-in question. This is a waste of time since you cannot grid a negative number.

(8) If your first attempt does not eliminate 3 of the 4 choices, try to choose a number that's of a different "type." Here are some examples of types:

　(a) A positive integer greater than 1.

　(b) A positive fraction (or decimal) between 0 and 1.

75

(c) A negative integer less than -1.

(d) A negative fraction (or decimal) between -1 and 0.

(9) If you are picking pairs of numbers try different combinations from (8). For example you can try two positive integers greater than 1, two negative integers less than -1, or one positive and one negative integer, etc.

Remember that these are just guidelines and there may be rare occasions where you might break these rules. For example sometimes it is so quick and easy to plug in 0 and/or 1 that you might do this even though only some of the answer choices get eliminated.

Try to answer the following question using this strategy. **Do not** check the solution until you have attempted this question yourself.

LEVEL 3: HEART OF ALGEBRA

1. Which of the following is equal to $\frac{x+66}{22}$?

(A) $\frac{x+33}{11}$

(B) $x + 3$

(C) $3x$

(D) $\frac{x}{22} + 3$

Solution by picking a number: Let's choose a value for x, say $x = 11$. We first substitute an 11 in for x into the given expression and use our calculator (if allowed). We type in the following: $(11 + 66)/22$ and we get $x = 3.5$. **Put a nice big, dark circle around this number so that you can find it easily later.** We now substitute 11 into each answer choice and use our calculator.

(A) $(11 + 33)/11 = 4$
(B) $11 + 3 = 14$
(C) $3*11 = 33$
(D) $11/22 + 3 = 3.5$

We now compare each of these numbers to the number that we put a nice big, dark circle around. Since (A), (B) and (C) are incorrect we can eliminate them. Therefore the answer is choice (D).

Important note: (D) is **not** the correct answer simply because it is equal to 3.5. It is correct because all 3 of the other choices are **not** 3.5. **You absolutely must check all four choices!**

As an example of how things could go wrong with incorrect reasoning, suppose we were to choose $x = 0$. Then the given expression becomes **3**, and the answer choices become

(A) 3
(B) 3
(C) 0
(D) 3

In this case we have eliminated (C), but (A), (B) and (D) are **all** potential solutions. A common error is to choose the first answer to come out correct. This is certainly a good guessing strategy, especially if you are running out of time, but it can potentially lead to the wrong answer. In this problem you might have chosen choice (A), and you would have gotten the answer wrong! This is also why we generally try not to pick numbers to be too simple. It often leads to multiple answer choices coming out to the correct number.

Before we go on, try to solve this problem algebraically.

Most students have no trouble at all adding two fractions with the same denominator. For example,

$$\frac{x}{22} + \frac{66}{22} = \frac{x+66}{22}$$

But these same students have trouble reversing this process.

$$\frac{x+66}{22} = \frac{x}{22} + \frac{66}{22}$$

Note that these two equations are **identical** except that the left and right hand sides have been switched. Note also that to break a fraction into two (or more) pieces, the original denominator is repeated for **each** piece.

* Algebraic solution: An algebraic solution to the above problem consists of the following quick computation

$$\frac{x+66}{22} = \frac{x}{22} + \frac{66}{22} = \frac{x}{22} + 3$$

77

This is choice (D).

Let's practice some more. Try to solve each of the following problems. First use the strategy of picking numbers discussed above. Then, if possible, solve each problem another way. The answers to these problems, followed by full solutions are at the end of this lesson. **Do not** look at the answers until you have attempted these problems yourself. Please remember to mark off any problems you get wrong.

LEVEL 1: HEART OF ALGEBRA

2. Dawn is selling $5d$ CDs at a price of p dollars each. If x is the number of CDs she did <u>not</u> sell, which of the following represents the total dollar amount she received in sales from the CDs?

    (A) $px - 5d$
    (B) $5d - px$
    (C) $p(x - 5d)$
    (D) $p(5d - x)$

3. Which of the following expressions is equivalent to 7 less than the product of x and y?

    (A) $x + y - 7$
    (B) $xy - 7$
    (C) $7xy$
    (D) $7(x - y)$

4. If $a \times b = 2b$ for all values of b, what is the value of a?

    (A) $-b$
    (B) -2
    (C) 2
    (D) b

78

LEVEL 2: HEART OF ALGEBRA

5. Which of the following is an expression for 25 less than the product of y and 7?

    (A) $7y - 25$
    (B) $25 - 7y$
    (C) $(y + 7) - 25$
    (D) $7(y - 25)$

6. If $\frac{y}{z} = -3$, then $y + 3z =$

    (A) -1
    (B) 0
    (C) 1
    (D) y

LEVEL 3: HEART OF ALGEBRA

7. If $(\sqrt{x})^k = 5$, what is the value of $\frac{1}{x^k}$?

8. If $\frac{x}{y} = \frac{3}{r}$, which of the following must equal 3?

    (A) x

    (B) y

    (C) $\frac{y}{x}$

    (D) $\frac{xr}{y}$

9. If x is $\frac{3}{5}$ of y and y is $\frac{5}{7}$ of z, what is the value of $\frac{z}{x}$?

    (A) $\frac{7}{3}$

    (B) $\frac{10}{7}$

    (C) $\frac{5}{4}$

    (D) $\frac{3}{7}$

LEVEL 4: HEART OF ALGEBRA

10. If $y = 3^x$, which of the following expressions is equivalent to $9^x - 3^{x+2}$ for all positive integer values of x ?

(A) $3y - 3$
(B) $y^2 - y$
(C) $y^2 - 3y$
(D) $y^2 - 9y$

Answers

1. D	6. B
2. D	7. 1/25 or .04
3. B	8. D
4. C	9. A
5. A	10.D

Note: The full solution for question 5 has been omitted because it is very similar to the solution to question 3.

Full Solutions

2.

Solution by picking numbers: Let's try $d = 4$, $p = 2$, $x = 5$. In this case Dawn is selling 20 CDs at a price of 2 dollars each. She did not sell 5 of them. Thus, she sold 15 of them and therefore she made $15 \cdot 2 = \mathbf{30}$ dollars. **Put a nice big, dark circle around this number so that you can find it easily later.** We now substitute the numbers that we chose into each answer choice.

(A) $2 * 5 - 5 * 4 = 10 - 20 = -10$
(B) $5 * 4 - 2 * 5 = 20 - 10 = 10$
(C) $2(5 - 5 * 4) = 2(5 - 20) = 2(-15) = -30$
(D) $2(5 * 4 - 5) = 2(20 - 5) = 2 * 15 = 30$

Since (A), (B) and (C) are incorrect we can eliminate them. Therefore the answer is choice (D).

Important note: (D) is **not** the correct answer simply because it is equal to 30. It is correct because all 3 of the other choices are **not** 30.

Remark: It is not necessary to finish a computation if the answer is clearly incorrect. For example, in choice (C) we could stop at $2(5 - 20)$ since this is clearly a negative number, and we know that the answer is positive.

* **Algebraic solution:** Dawn sold $(5d - x)$ CDs ($5d$ is the total and x is the number she did not sell). Thus the total dollar amount Dawn received in sales is $p(5d - x)$ (here p is the price per CD and $(5d - x)$ is the number of CDs that Dawn sold). Thus, the answer is choice (D).

3.

Solution by picking numbers: Let's choose values for x and y, say $x = 2$, $y = 6$. Then the product of x and y is $2 \cdot 6 = 12$. So 7 less than the product of x and y is $12 - 7 = 5$. **Put a nice big, dark circle around this number so that you can find it easily later.** We now substitute 2 for x and 6 for y into each answer choice and use our calculator.

      (A) $2 + 6 - 7 = 1$
      (B) $2 * 6 - 7 = 12 - 7 = 5$
      (C) $7 * 2 * 6 = 84$
      (D) $7(2 - 6) = 7(-4) = -28$

We now compare each of these numbers to the number that we put a nice big, dark circle around. Since (A), (C) and (D) are incorrect we can eliminate them. Therefore the answer is choice (B).

Important note: (B) is **not** the correct answer simply because it is equal to 5. It is correct because all 3 of the other choices are **not** 5. **You absolutely must check all four choices!**

* **A quick algebraic solution:** The product of x and y is xy, and so 7 less than the product of x and y is $xy - 7$, choice (B).

Common error: A common mistake is to write "7 less than xy" as $7 - xy$. This is incorrect. For example, 7 less than 8 is 1. It is **not** -1.

"7 less than 8" $= 8 - 7 = 1$.
"7 less than the product of x and y" = "7 less than xy" $= xy - 7$.

4.

Solution by picking numbers: Let's choose a value for b, say $b = 4$. Then the equation becomes $a \times 4 = 8$ or $4a = 8$, so that $a = 2$. **Put a nice big, dark circle around this number so that you can find it easily later.** With $b = 4$, notice that the answer choices become

(A) -4
(B) -2
(C) 2
(D) 4

Since (A), (B) and (D) are incorrect we can eliminate them. Therefore the answer is choice (C).

Important note: (C) is **not** the correct answer simply because it is equal to 2. It is correct because all 3 of the other choices are **not** 2.

* Algebraic solution: Simply divide each side of the equation by b to get $a = 2$. Thus, the answer is (C).

6.

Solution by picking numbers: Let's try $y = 6$ and $z = -2$. First note that $\frac{y}{z} = \frac{6}{-2} = -3$. Therefore our choices for y and z are acceptable. Now, $y + 3z = 6 + 3(-2) = 0$. This is choice (B).

* Algebraic solution: Multiplying each side of the equation by z gives us $y = -3z$. We now add $3z$ to each side to get $y + 3z = 0$, choice (B).

7.

* Solution by picking numbers: The nature of the question implies that every choice of k will lead to the same answer (see remark below for an exception). So choose $k = 1$. Then $\sqrt{x} = 5$, so that $x = 5^2 = 25$. Then $\frac{1}{x^k} = \frac{1}{x} = 1/25$ or $.04$.

Exception: We cannot choose $k = 0$ because the left side would then become 1 making the given equation $1 = 5$ which is false.

Algebraic solution: $\left(\sqrt{x}\right)^k = x^{\frac{k}{2}}$, so that the equation is $x^{\frac{k}{2}} = 5$. We square both sides to get $x^k = 25$. So $\frac{1}{x^k} = 1/25$ or $.04$.

For a review of negative and fractional exponents see the optional material at the end of this lesson.

8.

Solution by picking numbers: Before picking numbers put a nice big, dark circle around the number **3** in the problem. Now let's plug in values for x, y and r. Let's try the following.

$$r = 6 \quad x = 2 \quad y = 4$$

Notice that we chose the numbers so that they are all distinct, they are all simple but not too simple, and the given equation holds.

Now we substitute these values into each answer choice. Remember that we are looking for the answer to be 3.

(A) 2
(B) 4
(C) $4/2 = 2$
(D) $2 * 6/4 = 3$

We can eliminate choices (A), (B) and (C) since they did not come out to 3. Thus, the answer is choice (D).

* A quick algebraic solution: Simply multiply each side of the given equation by r to get 3 by itself. We get $\frac{xr}{y} = 3$, which is choice (D).

Another option that students seem to like: Many students seem to prefer cross multiplication followed by division so we show this computation here.

$$\frac{x}{y} = \frac{3}{r}$$
$$xr = 3y$$
$$\frac{xr}{y} = 3.$$

Note that cross multiplying actually creates an additional algebraic step, but the amount of time lost is very small, so it is okay if you prefer this.

9.

* Solution by picking a number: Let's choose a value for z, say $z = 35$ (this seems like a good choice since it is the product of the two denominators). Then

$$y = \frac{5}{7} \cdot 35 = 25 \text{ (the word "of" indicates multiplication)},$$

and $x = \frac{3}{5} \cdot 25 = 15$. Therefore, $\frac{z}{x} = \frac{35}{15} = \frac{7}{3}$, choice (A).

Recall: To reduce the fraction $\frac{35}{15}$ in you calculator, type 35/15, and then press MATH ENTER ENTER.

If a calculator is not allowed for the problem we have $\frac{35}{15} = \frac{7 \cdot 5}{3 \cdot 5} = \frac{7}{3}$.

Algebraic solution: $x = \frac{3y}{5}$ and $y = \frac{5z}{7}$. Solving the last equation for z gives us $z = \frac{7y}{5}$. Then

$$\frac{z}{x} = (\frac{7y}{5})/(\frac{3y}{5}) = (\frac{7y}{5}) \cdot (\frac{5}{3y}) = \frac{7}{3}.$$

Thus, the answer is choice (A).

10.

* Solution by picking a number: Let's choose a value for x, say $x = 2$. Then

$$y = 3^2 = 9, \text{ and } 9^x - 3^{x+2} = 9^2 - 3^4 = 0.$$

Put a nice big dark circle around the number 0. We now substitute $y = 9$ into each answer choice.

(A) $3 \cdot 9 - 3 = 27 - 3 = 24$
(B) $9^2 - 9 = 81 - 9 = 72$
(C) $9^2 - 3 \cdot 9 = 81 - 27 = 54$
(D) $9^2 - 9 \cdot 9 = 81 - 81 = 0$

Since (A), (B) and (C) are incorrect we can eliminate them. Therefore the answer is choice (D).

* Algebraic solution:

$$9^x - 3^{x+2} = (3^2)^x - 3^x 3^2 = (3^x)^2 - 9(3^x) = y^2 - 9y.$$

This is choice (D).

Note: For a review of the basic laws of exponents we used here see the Optional Material at the end of Lesson 5.

OPTIONAL MATERIAL

Negative and Fractional Exponents

Law	Example
$x^{-1} = 1/x$	$3^{-1} = 1/3$
$x^{-a} = 1/x^a$	$9^{-2} = 1/81$
$x^{1/n} = \sqrt[n]{x}$	$x^{1/3} = \sqrt[3]{x}$
$x^{m/n} = \sqrt[n]{x^m} = \left(\sqrt[n]{x}\right)^m$	$x^{9/2} = \sqrt{x^9} = \left(\sqrt{x}\right)^9$

Now let's practice. Rewrite each of the following expressions without negative or fractional exponents.

1. 7^{-1}

2. $\dfrac{5^2}{5^5}$

3. $\dfrac{x^{-5} \cdot x^{-3}}{x^{-4}}$

4. $5^{\frac{1}{2}}$

5. $5^{-\frac{1}{2}}$

6. $7^{-\frac{11}{3}}$

7. $\dfrac{x^{-\frac{5}{2}} \cdot x^{-1}}{x^{-\frac{4}{3}}}$

Answers

1. $\dfrac{1}{7}$

2. $5^{-3} = \dfrac{1}{5^3} = \dfrac{1}{125}$

3. $\dfrac{x^{-8}}{x^{-4}} = x^{-4} = \dfrac{1}{x^4}$

4. $\sqrt{5}$

5. $\dfrac{1}{5^{\frac{1}{2}}} = \dfrac{1}{\sqrt{5}}$

6. $\dfrac{1}{7^{\frac{11}{3}}} = \dfrac{1}{\sqrt[3]{7^{11}}}$

7. $\dfrac{x^{-\frac{7}{2}}}{x^{-\frac{4}{3}}} = x^{-\frac{13}{6}} = \dfrac{1}{x^{\frac{13}{6}}} = \dfrac{1}{\sqrt[6]{x^{13}}}$

Remark for number 5: In high school math classes, teachers will often insist that denominators of fractions be **rationalized**. This means that a legal operation should be performed to remove any radicals from the denominator. If we so choose we can do this in the solution to number 5 by multiplying the numerator and denominator by $\sqrt{5}$ to get $\dfrac{\sqrt{5}}{5}$.

Challenge problem: Rationalize the denominators in the solutions to questions 6 and 7.

Answers: 6. $\dfrac{\sqrt[3]{7^{22}}}{7^{11}}$ 7. $\dfrac{1}{\sqrt[6]{x^{13}}} = \dfrac{\sqrt[6]{x^{65}}}{x^{13}}$

LESSON 10
GEOMETRY

Reminder: Before beginning this lesson remember to redo the problems from Lessons 2 and 6 that you have marked off. Do not "unmark" a question unless you get it correct.

Turn to page 75 and review **Pick a number**. Then try to answer the following question using this strategy. **Do not** check the solution until you have attempted this question yourself.

LEVEL 2: GEOMETRY

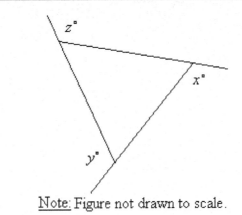

Note: Figure not drawn to scale.

1.   In the figure above, what is the value of $x + y + z$?

Solution by picking a number: Inside the triangle we can pick any 2 angles for free (just make sure that their sum is strictly less than 180). Here is an example:

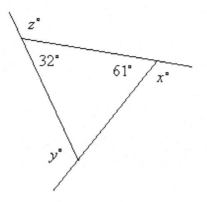

Since the angle measures of a triangle sum to 180, the other interior angle is

$$180 - 32 - 61 = 87 \text{ degrees.}$$

Furthermore, **the measure of an exterior angle to a triangle is the sum of the measures of the two opposite interior angles of the triangle.** So we have

$$x = 87 + 32 = 119$$
$$y = 32 + 61 = 93$$
$$z = 87 + 61 = 148$$

So, $x + y + z = 119 + 93 + 148 = \mathbf{360}$.

Alternative: Each exterior angle of the triangle forms a **linear pair** with its adjacent interior angle, and therefore these two angles are **supplementary**. So $x + 61 = 180$, and therefore $x = 180 - 61 = 119$. Similarly, $y = 180 - 87 = 93$ and $z = 180 - 32 = 148$.

So, $x + y + z = 119 + 93 + 148 = \mathbf{360}$.

Before we go on, try to solve this problem directly.

* Direct solution: A moment's thought will reveal that when we add x, y and z, we are adding each interior angle of the triangle twice (see bold text in the first solution above). Since there are 180 degrees in a triangle, the answer is $2 \cdot 180 = \mathbf{360.}$

Remark: We see from this solution that the answer to this problem is independent of what any of the interior angles are actually equal to.

Plug in the Given Point

If the graph of a function or other equation passes through certain points, plug those points into the equation to eliminate answer choices.

Try to answer the following question using this strategy. **Do not** check the solution until you have attempted this question yourself.

LEVEL 3: GEOMETRY

2. Which of the following is an equation of the line in the xy-plane that passes through the point $(0, -3)$ and is parallel to the line $y = -4x + 7$?

   (A) $4x + y = -6$
   (B) $4x + y = -3$
   (C) $4x + y = 3$
   (D) $-x + 4y = 3$

* Since the point $(0, -3)$ lies on the line, if we substitute 0 in for x and -3 for y, we should get a true equation

   (A) $4 \cdot 0 - 3 = -6$ or $-3 = -6$ False
   (B) $4 \cdot 0 - 3 = -3$ or $-3 = -3$ True
   (C) $4 \cdot 0 - 3 = 3$ or $-3 = 3$ False
   (D) $-0 + 4(-3) = 3$ or $-12 = 3$ False

We can eliminate choices (A), (C) and (D) because they have become false. The answer is therefore choice (B).

Important note: (B) is **not** the correct answer simply because it came out true. It is correct because all 3 of the other choices were false.

Before we go on, try to solve this problem using geometry.

Geometric solution: Recall the slope-intercept form for the equation of a line: $y = mx + b$

$(0, -3)$ is the y-intercept of the line. Thus, $b = -3$. The slope of the given line is -4. Since the new line is parallel to this line, its slope is also -4, and the equation of the new line in slope-intercept form is $y = -4x - 3$.

We now add $4x$ to each side of this last equation to get $4x + y = -3$. This is choice (B).

Recall: Parallel lines have the same slope, and perpendicular lines have slopes that are negative reciprocals of each other.

You're doing great! Let's practice a bit more. Try to solve each of the following problems by picking numbers or plugging in points. Then, if possible, solve each problem another way. The answers to these problems, followed by full solutions are at the end of this lesson. **Do not look at the answers until you have attempted these problems yourself.** Please remember to mark off any problems you get wrong.

LEVEL 1: GEOMETRY

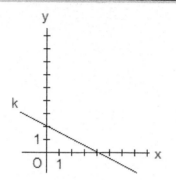

3. What is the equation of line k in the figure above?

   (A) $y = -2x + 2$
   (B) $y = -2x + 4$
   (C) $y = -\frac{1}{2}x + 2$
   (D) $y = -\frac{1}{2}x + 4$

LEVEL 2: GEOMETRY

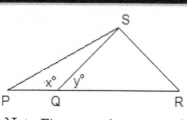

Note: Figure not drawn to scale.

4. In the figure above, point Q lies on side PR. If $50 < y < 52$, what is one possible value of x?

LEVEL 3: GEOMETRY

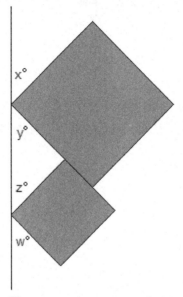

: Figure not drawn to scale.

5. In the figure above, the two shaded regions are squares. Which of the following must be true?

    (A) $x = y$
    (B) $x = w$
    (C) $y = z$
    (D) $y = w$

: Figure not drawn to scale.

6. In the triangle above, y is an integer. If $37 < x < 40$, what is one possible value of y ?

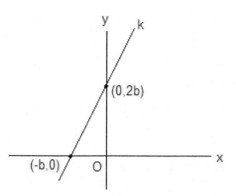

7.   In the figure above, what is the slope of line k ?

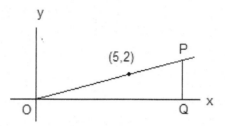

8.   Line k (not shown) passes through O and intersects PQ between P and Q. What is one possible value of the slope of line k?

Definitions Used in This Lesson

Definitions of a **triangle**, **quadrilateral**, **rectangle**, and **square** can be found on page 29.

Two angles form a **linear pair** if they are **adjacent** and **supplementary**. Two angles are **supplementary** if their measures add up to 180 degrees.

Formulas Used in This Lesson

The sum of the measures in degrees of the angles of a triangle is 180.

The **slope** of a line is

$$\text{Slope} = m = \frac{rise}{run} = \frac{y_2 - y_1}{x_2 - x_1}$$

Lines with positive slope have graphs that go upwards from left to right. Lines with negative slope have graphs that go downwards from left to right. If the slope of a line is zero, it is horizontal. Vertical lines have **no** slope (also known as **infinite** slope or **undefined** slope).

91

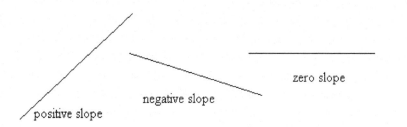

zero slope

negative slope

positive slope

no slope

The **slope-intercept form of an equation of a line** is $y = mx + b$ where m is the slope of the line and b is the y-coordinate of the y-intercept, i.e. the point $(0, b)$ is on the line. Note that this point lies on the y-axis.

Answers

1. 360
2. B
3. C
4. 129

5. D
6. 101, 102,..., 105
7. 2
8. $0 < m < .4$

Full Solutions

3.

Solution by plugging in the point: Since the point $(0, 2)$ lies on the line, if we substitute 0 in for x, we should get 2 for y. Let's substitute 0 in for x into each answer choice.

(A) 2
(B) 4
(C) 2
(D) 4

We can eliminate choices (B) and (D) because they did not come out to 2.

The point $(4, 0)$ also lies on the line. So if we substitute 4 in for x, we should get 0 for y. Let's substitute 4 in for x in choices (A) and (C).

(A) $-2(4) + 2 = -8 + 2 = -6$
(C) $(-\frac{1}{2})(4) + 2 = -2 + 2 = 0$

We can eliminate choice (A) because it did not come out to 0. Therefore the answer is choice (C).

* Solution using the slope-intercept form of an equation of a line: Recall that the slope-intercept form for the equation of a line is

$$y = mx + b.$$

$(0,2)$ is the y-intercept of the line. Thus, $b = 2$. The slope of the given line is $m = \dfrac{rise}{run} = -\dfrac{2}{4} = -\dfrac{1}{2}$. Therefore the equation of the line is $y = -\dfrac{1}{2}x + 2$, choice (C).

Note: To find the slope using the graph we simply note that to get from the y-intercept of the line to the x-intercept of the line we need to move down 2, then right 4

4.

* Solution by picking a number: Let's choose a value for y, the easiest choice being $y = 51$. Then $x = 180 - 51 = \mathbf{129}$.

Remark: Angles PQS and SQR form a **linear pair**. This means that they are **supplementary**, ie. their measures add up to 180 degrees. This is why $x = 180 - y$.

Complete geometric solution: $180 - 50 = 130$ and $180 - 52 = 128$. Therefore $128 < x < 130$. So a possible answer is **129**.

Note: Although there are infinitely many solutions to this question, there is only one answer that will fit in the grid, namely 129.

5.

Solution by picking a number: Let's choose a value for x, say $x = 35$. Since each angle of a square measures 90 degrees, $x + y = 90$. Therefore, $y = 90 - x = 90 - 35 = 55$. Similarly we have that $z = 90 - y = 90 - 55 = 35$, and $w = 90 - z = 90 - 35 = 55$.

To summarize, $x = z = 35$ and $y = w = 55$. Now let's check if each answer choice is true or false.

      (A) False
      (B) False
      (C) False
      (D) True

Since (A), (B) and (C) are each false we can eliminate them. The answer is therefore choice (D).

* Complete geometric solution: As described in the previous solution, we have $x + y = 90$, $y + z = 90$, and $z + w = 90$.

We only need the last two of these equations. Simply subtract the two equations (in either order).

$$\begin{aligned} y + z &= 90 \\ z + w &= 90 \\ \hline y - w &= 0 \end{aligned}$$

Therefore $y = w$, choice (D).

Clarification of the computation:

$$(y + z) - (z + w) = y + z - z - w = y - w.$$

Caution: Make sure you distribute that minus sign correctly!

6.

* Solution by picking a number: Let's choose a value for x, say $x = 38$. Then $y = 180 - x - x = 180 - 38 - 38 = \mathbf{104}$.

Complete geometric solution: We have $180 - 37 - 37 = 106$ and $180 - 40 - 40 = 100$. Therefore $100 < y < 106$. So we can grid in **101, 102, 103, 104**, or **105**.

7.

Solution by picking a number: Let's choose a value for b, say $b = 3$. Then the two points are $(-3, 0)$ and $(0, 6)$. The slope is $\frac{6-0}{0-(-3)} = \frac{6}{3} = \mathbf{2}$.

Remarks: (1) Here we have used the slope formula $m = \frac{y_2 - y_1}{x_2 - x_1}$.

(2) $0 - (-3) = 0 + 3 = 3$

(3) We could have also found the slope graphically by plotting the two points and observing that to get from $(-3, 0)$ to $(0, 6)$ we need to move up 6 and right 3. Thus, the slope is $m = \frac{rise}{run} = \frac{6}{3} = 2$.

* Solution using the slope formula: Let's use the formula for slope (as given in Remark (1) above). $\frac{2b-0}{0-(-b)} = \frac{2b}{b} = \mathbf{2}$.

8.

* Solution by picking a line: Let's choose a specific line k. The easiest choice is the line passing through $(0,0)$ and $(5,1)$. Now plug these two points into the slope formula to get $\frac{1-0}{5-0} = \mathbf{1/5}$.

Remarks: (1) Here we have used the slope formula $m = \frac{y_2-y_1}{x_2-x_1}$.

(2) If the line j passes through the origin (the point $(0,0)$) and the point (a,b) with $a \neq 0$, then the slope of line j is simply $\frac{b}{a}$.

Complete geometric solution: The slope of line OP is $\frac{2}{5} = .4$ (see Remark (2) above) and the slope of line OQ is 0. Therefore we can choose any number strictly between 0 and $.4$ that fits in the answer grid.

OPTIONAL MATERIAL

Point-slope Equation of a Line

The point-slope form for an equation of a line is $y - y_0 = m(x - x_0)$ where m is the slope of the line and (x_0, y_0) is any point on the line.

Example: Write an equation of the line with slope 3 that passes through the point $(5, -2)$.

Solution using point-slope form: In this example $m = 3$, $x_0 = 5$, $y_0 = -2$. So the equation is $y - (-2) = 3(x - 5)$, or $y + 2 = 3(x - 5)$.

Note: If we wish to put the line into slope-intercept form, we simply solve the equation for y. First distribute the 3 on the right hand side to get $y + 2 = 3x - 15$. Then subtract 2 from each side of the equation to get $y = 3x - 17$.

Now you try one.

Example: Write an equation of the line with slope -2 that passes through the point $(-4, 3)$.

Answer

Point-slope form: $y - 3 = -2(x + 4)$

Slope-Intercept form: $y = -2x - 5$

LESSON 11
PASSPORT TO ADVANCED MATH

Reminder: Before beginning this lesson remember to redo the problems from Lessons 3 and 7 that you have marked off. Do not "unmark" a question unless you get it correct.

Graphs of Functions

If f is a function, then

$f(a) = b$ is equivalent to "the point (a, b) lies on the graph of f."

Example 1:

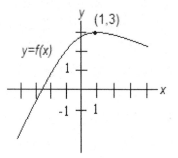

In the figure above we see that the point $(1,3)$ lies on the graph of the function f. Therefore $f(1) = 3$.

Try to answer the following question using this fact. **Do not** check the solution until you have attempted this question yourself.

LEVEL 3: ADVANCED MATH

1. The function k is defined by $k(x) = 2x^2 + bx - 3$, where b is a constant. In the xy-plane, the graph of $y = k(x)$ crosses the x-axis where $x = 3$. What is the value of b ?

   (A) 5
   (B) 3
   (C) −3
   (D) −5

* A graph crosses the x-axis at a point where $y = 0$. Thus, the point $(3,0)$ is on the graph of $y = k(x)$. Equivalently, $k(3) = 0$. So

$$0 = 2 \cdot 3^2 + b(3) - 3$$
$$0 = 2 \cdot 9 + 3b - 3$$
$$0 = 18 + 3b - 3$$
$$0 = 15 + 3b$$
$$-3b = 15$$
$$b = \frac{15}{-3} = -5.$$

This is choice (D).

Function Facts

Fact 1: The **y-intercept** of the graph of a function $y = f(x)$ is the point on the graph where $x = 0$ (if it exists). There can be at most one y-intercept for the graph of a function. A y-intercept has the form $(0, b)$ for some real number b. Equivalently, $f(0) = b$.

Fact 2: An **x-intercept** of the graph of a function is a point on the graph where $y = 0$. There can be more than one x-intercept for the graph of a function or none at all. An x-intercept has the form $(a, 0)$ for some real number a. Equivalently, $f(a) = 0$.

Example 2:

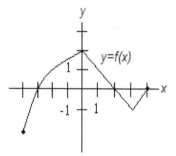

In the figure above we see that the graph of f has y-intercept $(0,2)$ and x-intercepts $(-3,0)$, $(2,0)$ and $(4,0)$.

The numbers -3, 2, and 4 are also called **zeros**, **roots**, or **solutions** of the function.

Note that in example 2 we have $f(-3) = 0$, $f(2) = 0$, and $f(4) = 0$.

Fact 3: If the graph of $f(x)$ is above the x-axis, then $f(x) > 0$. If the graph of f is below the x-axis, then $f(x) < 0$. If the graph of f is higher than the graph of g, then $f(x) > g(x)$.

97

Example 3: In the figure for example 2 above, observe that $f(x) < 0$ for $-4 \leq x < -3$ and $2 < x < 4$. Also observe that $f(x) > 0$ for $-3 < x < 2$.

Fact 4: The graph of a function always passes the **vertical line test**: any vertical line can hit the graph *at most* once.

For example, a circle is *never* the graph of a function. It always fails the vertical line test as shown in the figure below.

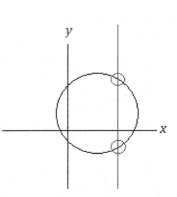

Now try to solve each of the following problems. The answers to these problems, followed by full solutions are at the end of this lesson. **Do not** look at the answers until you have attempted these problems yourself. Please remember to mark off any problems you get wrong.

LEVEL 1: ADVANCED MATH

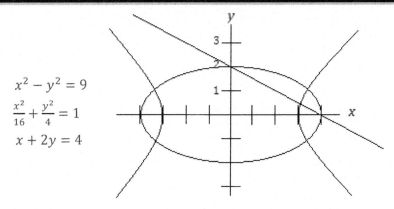

$$x^2 - y^2 = 9$$
$$\frac{x^2}{16} + \frac{y^2}{4} = 1$$
$$x + 2y = 4$$

2. A system of three equations in two unknowns and their graphs in the xy-plane are shown above. How many solutions does the system have?

98

3. Which of the following graphs could not be the graph of a function?

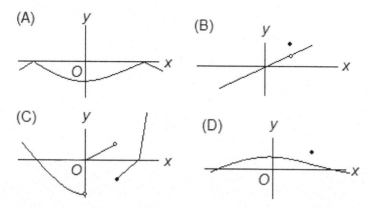

(A)

(B)

(C)

(D)

LEVEL 3: ADVANCED MATH

4. The function g is defined by $g(x) = -2x^2 - cx + d$, where c and d are constants. In the xy-plane, the graph of $y = h(x)$ crosses the x-axis where $x = 1$. What is the value of $d - c$?

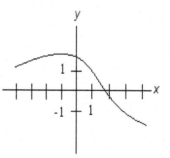

5. The figure above shows the graph of the function k. Which of the following is greater than $k(1)$?

   (A) $k(-3)$
   (B) $k(2)$
   (C) $k(3)$
   (D) $k(4)$

6. In the xy-plane, the graph of the function g has x-intercepts at $-5, -2, 2,$ and 5. Which of the following could define g ?

(A) $g(x) = (x - 5)^2(x - 2)^2$
(B) $g(x) = (x + 5)^2(x + 2)^2$
(C) $g(x) = (x - 5)^2(x + 2)(x - 2)^3(x + 5)$
(D) $g(x) = (x - 5)(x + 5)(x - 2)^2$

7. In the xy-plane, the graph of the function f, with equation $f(x) = cx^2 - 7$, passes through the point $(-3, 38)$. What is the value of c?

LEVEL 4: ADVANCED MATH

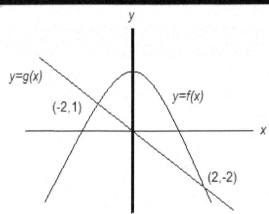

8. In the xy-plane above, the graph of the function f is a parabola, and the graph of the function g is a line. The graphs of f and g intersect at $(-2,1)$ and $(2,-2)$. For which of the following values of x is $f(x) - g(x) < 0$?

(A) -3
(B) -1
(C) 0
(D) 1

Answers

1. D	5. A
2. 0	6. C
3. D	7. 5
4. 2	8. A

Full Solutions

2.

* Solution by looking at the graph: There is no point that is common to all three graphs. So the system has no solutions. The answer is **0**.

Notes: (1) A solution to the system of equations is a point that satisfies all three equations simultaneously. Graphically this means that the point is on all three graphs. Although there are several points that are common to two of the graphs, there are none that are common to all three.

(2) The graph of the equation $x^2 - y^2 = 9$ is the **hyperbola** in the figure above with **vertices** $(-3,0)$ and $(3,0)$.

(3) The graph of the equation $\frac{x^2}{16} + \frac{y^2}{4} = 1$ is the **ellipse** in the figure above with vertices $(-4,0)$, $(4,0)$, $(0,2)$, and $(0,-2)$.

(4) The graph of the equation $x + 2y = 4$ is the **line** in the figure above with **intercepts** $(4,0)$ and $(0,2)$.

$(4,0)$ is the **x-intercept** of the line, and $(0,2)$ is the **y-intercept** of the line.

(5) Consider the following system of equations:

$$\frac{x^2}{16} + \frac{y^2}{4} = 1$$
$$x + 2y = 4$$

This system has the two solutions $(0,2)$ and $(4,0)$. These are the two points common to the graphs of these two equations (the ellipse and the line), also known as **points of intersection** of the two graphs.

(6) Consider the following system of equations:

$$x^2 - y^2 = 9$$
$$x + 2y = 4$$

This system also has two solutions. These are the two points common to the hyperbola and the line. Finding these two solutions requires solving the system algebraically, which we won't do here.

One of these solutions can be seen on the graph. It looks to be approximately $(3.1, 0.5)$.

The second solution does not appear on the portion of the graph that is displayed. If we continued to graph the line and hyperbola to the left we would see them intersect one more time.

(6) Consider the following system of equations:

$$x^2 - y^2 = 9$$
$$\frac{x^2}{16} + \frac{y^2}{4} = 1$$

This system has four solutions. These are the four points common to the hyperbola and the ellipse. Finding these four solutions requires solving the system algebraically, which we won't do here. These solutions can be seen clearly on the graph.

3.
* Only choice (D) fails the **vertical line test**. In other words, we can draw a vertical line that hits the graph more than once:

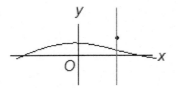

So the answer is choice (D).

4.
* A graph crosses the x-axis at a point where $y = 0$. Thus, the point $(1, 0)$ is on the graph of $y = g(x)$. Equivalently, $g(1) = 0$. So,

$$0 = g(1) = -2(1)^2 - c + d = -2 + d - c.$$

We add 2 to each side of this equation to get $d - c = 2$.

5.
* Let's draw a horizontal line through the point $(1, k(1))$. To do this start on the x-axis at 1 and go straight up until you hit the curve. This height is $k(1)$. Now draw a horizontal line through this point.

102

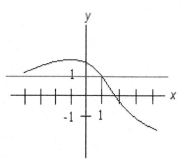

Now, notice that the graph is above this line when $x = -3$. So $k(-3)$ is greater than $k(1)$. So the answer is choice (A).

6.

* Solution by plugging in the points: $(-5,0)$, $(-2,0)$, $(2,0)$, and $(5,0)$ are on the graph of g. Thus, $g(-5) = g(-2) = g(2) = g(5) = 0$.

We can eliminate choices (A) and (D) by substituting -2 for x, and we can eliminate choice (B) by substituting 2 for x. The answer is therefore choice (C).

Remark: The **factor theorem** says that r is a root of the polynomial $p(x)$ if and only if $x - r$ is a factor of the polynomial.

In this question -5, -2, 2, and 0 are all roots of g. It follows that $x + 5$, $x + 2$, $x - 2$, and $x - 5$ are factors of g. Only choice (C) has all of these factors.

7.

* Solution: Since the graph of f passes through the point $(-3,38)$, $f(-3) = 38$. But by direct computation

$$f(-3) = c(-3)^2 - 7 = 9c - 7.$$

So $9c - 7 = 38$. Therefore $9c = 38 + 7 = 45$, and so $c = \frac{45}{9} = \textbf{5}$.

8.

Solution by starting with choice (C): Let's add some information to the picture.

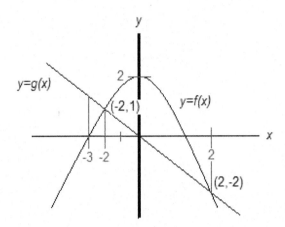

Now let's start with choice (C). Since the point $(0,2)$ is on the graph of f, we have that $f(0) = 2$. Since the point $(0,0)$ is on the graph of g, we have $g(0) = 0$. So $f(0) - g(0) = 2 - 0 = 2 > 0$. So we can eliminate choice (C).

A moment's thought should lead you to suspect that choice (A) might be the answer (if you do not see this it is okay – just keep trying answer choices until you get there). Since the point $(-3,0)$ is on the graph of f, we have $f(-3) = 0$. It looks like $(-3,1.5)$ is on the graph of g, so that $g(-3) = 1.5$. So $f(-3) - g(-3) = 0 - 1.5 = -1.5 < 0$. Thus, the answer is choice (A).

* Geometric solution: $f(x) - g(x) < 0$ is equivalent to $f(x) < g(x)$. Graphically this means that $f(x)$ is lower than $g(x)$. This happens at $x = -3$, choice (A).

Remark: If $-2 < x < 2$, then the graph of f is higher than the graph of g. This means that $f(x) > g(x)$, or equivalently $f(x) - g(x) > 0$. If $x < -2$ or $x > 2$, then the graph of f is lower than the graph of g. This means that $f(x) < g(x)$, or equivalently $f(x) - g(x) < 0$.

LESSON 12
PROBLEM SOLVING

Reminder: Before beginning this lesson remember to redo the problems from Lessons 4 and 8 that you have marked off. Do not "unmark" a question unless you get it correct.

Percent = "Out of 100"

Since the word percent means "out of 100," use the number 100 for totals in percent problems. This is just a specific example of the strategy of picking numbers from Lesson 9.

Try to answer the following question using the number 100. **Do not** check the solution until you have attempted this question yourself.

LEVEL 4: PROBLEM SOLVING

1. A person cuts a cake into n equal pieces and eats two pieces. In terms of n, what percent of the cake is left?

    (A) $100(n-2)\%$
    (B) $\frac{100(n-2)}{n}\%$
    (C) $\frac{100n}{n-2}\%$
    (D) $\frac{n-2}{100}\%$

* **Solution by picking a number:** Let's choose a value for n. Since this is a percent problem we will choose $n = 100$. So the person eats 2 pieces of the cake and there are 98 pieces left. Since there were 100 pieces total, the answer is **98%**. We now substitute our chosen value of n into each answer choice.

    (A) 100*98 = 9800%
    (B) 100*98/100 = 98%
    (C) 100*100/98 ≈ 102.04 %
    (D) 98/100 = 0.98%

Since (A), (C) and (D) are incorrect we can eliminate them. Therefore the answer is choice (B).

You should also try to solve this problem algebraically.

* Algebraic solution: The total number of pieces of cake is n. Since 2 pieces have been eaten, it follows that $n - 2$ have not been eaten. To get the **fraction** of cake that has not been eaten we divide the **number** of pieces that have not been eaten by the total. This is $\frac{n-2}{n}$. To change this to a **percent** we multiply by 100, to get $\frac{100(n-2)}{n}$ %, choice (B).

Note: The last step in the algebraic solution is equivalent to the usual ratio computation where we are changing the denominator to 100.

pieces not eaten	$n - 2$	x
total no. of pieces	n	100

$$\frac{n - 2}{n} = \frac{x}{100}$$
$$100(n - 2) = nx$$
$$\frac{100(n - 2)}{n} = x$$

Percent Change

Memorize the following simple formula for percent change problems.

$$Percent\ Change = \frac{Change}{Original} \times 100$$

Note that this is the same formula for both a percent increase and a percent decrease problem.

LEVEL 2: PROBLEM SOLVING

2. In September, Maria was able to type 30 words per minute. In October she was able to type 42 words per minute. By what percent did Maria's speed increase from September to October? (Disregard the percent symbol when gridding in your answer.)

* This is a percent increase problem. So we will use the formula for percent change.

The **original** value is 30. The new value is 42, so that the **change** is 12. Using the percent change formula, we get that the percent increase is $\frac{12}{30} \cdot 100 = 40\%$. So we grid in **40.**

Warning: Do not accidently use the new value for "change" in the formula. The **change** is the positive difference between the original and new values.

Now try to solve each of the following problems involving percents. The answers to these problems, followed by full solutions are at the end of this lesson. **Do not** look at the answers until you have attempted these problems yourself. Please remember to mark off any problems you get wrong.

LEVEL 1: PROBLEM SOLVING

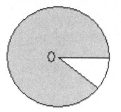

3. O is the center of the circle above. Approximately what percent of the circle is shaded?

    (A) 25%
    (B) 50%
    (C) 75%
    (D) 90%

LEVEL 2: PROBLEM SOLVING

4. 30 percent of 50 is 10 percent of what number?

5. If x is 40% of z and y is 55% of z, what is $x + y$ in terms of z?

    (A) $.95z$
    (B) $.85z$
    (C) $.75z$
    (D) $.65z$

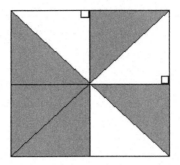

6.　* What percent of the square above is shaded?

    (A)　25%

    (B)　$33\frac{1}{3}$%

    (C)　50%

    (D)　$62\frac{1}{2}$%

7.　* At Sarak High School, approximately 3 percent of enrolled freshman, 6 percent of enrolled sophomores, and 8 percent of enrolled juniors scored more than 1300 on their PSAT in October 2015. If there were 412 freshman, 562 sophomores, and 614 juniors at Sarak High School in 2015, which of the following is closest to the total number of freshmen, sophomores, and juniors at Sarak High School who scored more than 1300 on their PSAT?

    (A)　72
    (B)　95
    (C)　98
    (D)　126

LEVEL 3: PROBLEM SOLVING

8.　What percent of 60 is 24? (Disregard the percent symbol when gridding in your answer.)

9.　During a sale at a retail store, if a customer buys one t-shirt at full price, the customer is given a 40 percent discount on a second t-shirt of equal or lesser value. If John buys two t-shirts that have full prices of $70 and $90, by what percent is the total cost of the two t-shirts reduced during the sale? (Disregard the percent symbol when you grid your answer.)

LEVEL 4: PROBLEM SOLVING

10. * If $x > 0$, then 3 percent of 11 percent of $8x$ equals what percent of x? (Disregard the percent symbol when you grid your answer.)

Answers

1. B
2. 40
3. D
4. 150
5. A

6. D
7. B
8. 40
9. 35/2 or 17.5
10. 2.64

Full Solutions

3.

* We can assume that the figure is drawn to scale (see Lesson 14). The answer is certainly more than 75%. Thus, the answer must be choice (D).

Clarification: If you are having trouble seeing that the answer is more than 75% just look at the following figure.

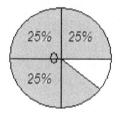

4.

* 30 percent of 50 is equal to $(0.3)(50) = 15$. So the question now becomes "15 is 10% of what number?" Well, 15 is 10% of **150**.

Algebraic solution: We begin by changing the English symbol to a mathematical equation. The word "percent" means "out of 100," the word "of" means "·," the word "is" means "=," and we replace the word "what" by the variable x.

$$\frac{30}{100} \cdot 50 = \frac{10}{100} \cdot x$$

$$\frac{15}{1} = \frac{x}{10}$$

Now cross multiply to get $x = \mathbf{150}$.

    5.

Solution by picking a number: Let's substitute the number 100 in for z. Then y is 55% of 100 which is 55, and x is 40% of 100 which is 40. Thus, $x + y = 40 + 55 = \mathbf{95}$. The answer is clearly choice (A), but for the sake of completion let's plug $z = 100$ into each answer choice.

        (A) 95
        (B) 85
        (C) 75
        (D) 65

We see that the answer is choice (A).

* An algebraic solution: $x = .40z$ and $y = .55z$. So we have that $x + y = .40z + .55z = .95z$. Therefore the answer is choice (A).

    6.

* 5 of the 8 pieces are shaded and each of these pieces has equal area.

$$\frac{5}{8} = .625 = 62.5\%, \text{ choice (D).}$$

Notes: (1) To change $\frac{5}{8}$ to the decimal $.625$ simply divide 5 by 8 in your calculator.

(2) To change the decimal to a percent move the decimal point two places to the right.

    7.

* $(.03)(412) + (.06)(562) + (.08)(614) = 95.2$. So the answer is choice (B).

    8.

* The word "what" indicates an unknown, let's call it x. The word percent means "out of 100" or "divided by 100." The word "of" indicates multiplication, and the word "is" indicates an equal sign. So we translate the given sentence into an algebraic equation as follows.

$$\frac{x}{100} \cdot 60 = 24$$

So $x = 24(\frac{100}{60}) = \mathbf{40}$.

9.

* Solution using the percent change formula: This is a percent decrease problem. So we will use the formula for percent change. The **original** cost of the 2 t-shirts is $70 + 90 = 160$. The new cost is $42 + 90 = 132$. Thus, the **change** is $160 - 132 = 28$. So the percent change is $\frac{28}{160} \cdot 100 = 17.5\%$. So we grid the answer **17.5**.

Note: To get the 42 in the second computation we need to discount 70 by 40 percent. Here are two ways to do that.

(1) We can compute 40% of $70 = .4 \cdot 70 = 28$, and then subtract $70 - 28 = 42$.

(2) We can compute 60% of $70 = .6 \cdot 70 = 42$ (taking a 40% discount of something is the same as taking 60% of that thing).

Warning: Do not accidently use the new value for "change" in the formula. The **change** is the positive difference between the original and new values.

10.

Solution by picking a number: Since this is a percent problem let's choose $x = 100$. Then 11 percent of $8x$ is 11 percent of 800 which is $(.11)(800) = 88$. 3 percent of 11 percent of $8x$ is 3 percent of 88 which is $(.03)(88) = 2.64$. Since we began with $x = 100$, the answer is 2.64.

* Direct solution: 3% of 11% of $8x$ is $(.03)(.11)(8x) = .0264x$ which is 2.64 percent of x. So we grid in $\mathbf{2.64}$.

OPTIONAL MATERIAL

The following questions will test your understanding of definitions used in this lesson. These are **not** SAT questions.

1. Convert each fraction to a decimal and a percent (round each result to two decimal places).

$$\frac{1}{2} \qquad \frac{1}{5} \qquad \frac{1}{3} \qquad 1 \qquad \frac{5}{3}$$

2. Convert each decimal to a percent and a reduced fraction.

$$.5 \quad .24 \quad 1 \quad 1.5 \quad 12$$

3. Convert each percent to a decimal and a reduced fraction.

$$5\% \quad .3\% \quad .07\% \quad 15\% \quad 100\%$$

Answers

1. $\frac{1}{2} = .5 = 50\%, \frac{1}{5} = .2 = 20\%, \frac{1}{3} = .33 = 33.33\%,$
   $1 = 1 = 100\%, \frac{5}{3} = 1.67 = 166.67\%$

2. $.5 = 50\% = \frac{1}{2}, .24 = 24\% = \frac{6}{25}, 1 = 100\% = 1,$
   $1.5 = 150\% = \frac{3}{2}, 12 = 1200\% = 12$

3. $5\% = .05 = \frac{1}{20}, .3\% = .003 = \frac{3}{1000}, .07\% = .0007 = \frac{7}{10,000},$
   $15\% = .15 = \frac{3}{20}, 100\% = 1 = 1$

LESSON 13
HEART OF ALGEBRA

Reminder: Before beginning this lesson remember to redo the problems from Lessons 1, 5 and 9 that you have marked off. Do not "unmark" a question unless you get it correct.

Try a Simple Operation

Problems that ask for an expression involving more than one variable often look much harder than they are. By performing a single operation, the problem is often reduced to one that is very easy to solve. The most common operations to try are addition, subtraction, multiplication and division.

Try to answer the following question using this strategy. **Do not** check the solution until you have attempted this question yourself.

LEVEL 2: HEART OF ALGEBRA

1. If $7x + y = 6$ and $5x + y = 2$, what is the value of $6x + y$?

* Solution by trying a simple operation: We add the two equations:

$$
\begin{array}{r}
7x + y = 6 \\
\underline{5x + y = 2} \\
12x + 2y = 8
\end{array}
$$

Now observe that $12x + 2y = 2(6x + y)$. So $6x + y = \dfrac{8}{2} = \mathbf{4}$.

Before we go on, try to solve this problem the way you would do it in school.

Solution using the elimination method: We subtract the two equations to isolate x

$$
\begin{array}{r}
7x + y = 6 \\
\underline{5x + y = 2} \\
2x = 4
\end{array}
$$

So $x = 2$. Substituting $x = 2$ back into the first equation we get

$$7(2) + y = 6$$
$$14 + y = 6$$
$$y = -8$$

So, $6x + y = 6(2) - 8 = 12 - 8 = \textbf{4}$.

Remark: This method of solution is explained in more detail in the optional material at the end of this lesson.

You're doing great! Let's just practice a bit more. Try to solve each of the following problems by using the strategy you just learned. Then, if possible, solve each problem another way. The answers to these problems, followed by full solutions are at the end of this lesson. **Do not** look at the answers until you have attempted these problems yourself. Please remember to mark off any problems you get wrong.

LEVEL 2: HEART OF ALGEBRA

2. If $x + 7y = 15$ and $x + 3y = 7$, what is the value of $x + 5y$?

3. If $\frac{a+3}{5} = 20$ and $\frac{a+b}{12} = 10$, what is the value of b?

LEVEL 3: HEART OF ALGEBRA

4. If $21x + 49y = 28$, what is the value of $3x + 7y$?

$5z$	$2z$
4	4
$4t$	w
8	8
$+9$	$+9$
52	34

5. In the correctly worked addition problems above, what is the value of $3z + 4t - w$?

6. If $ab = 4$, $bc = \frac{1}{3}$, $b^2 = 2$, what is the value of ac?

LEVEL 4: HEART OF ALGEBRA

$$ax + by = 25$$
$$ax + (b + 1)y = 35$$

7. Based on the equations above, which of the following must be true?

    (A) $x = 15$
    (B) $x = 20$
    (C) $y = 5$
    (D) $y = 10$

LEVEL 5: HEART OF ALGEBRA

8. If $xy = 6, yz = 10, xz = 15$, and $x > 0$, then $xyz =$

9. * If $5x = 1 + 4y$ and $6x = 2 - 3y$, what is the value of x?

10. If $x^{12} = \frac{3}{z}$ and $x^{11} = \frac{3y}{z}$ which of the following is an expression for x in terms of y?

    (A) $3y$

    (B) $2y$

    (C) y

    (D) $\frac{1}{y}$

Answers

1. 4	6. 2/3, .666, or .667
2. 11	7. D
3. 23	8. 30
4. 4	9. .282
5. 18	10. D

Full Solutions

2.
* Solution by trying a simple operation: We add the two equations

$$x + 7y = 15$$
$$\underline{x + 3y = 7}$$
$$2x + 10y = 22$$

Now observe that $2x + 10y = 2(x + 5y)$. So $x + 5y = \frac{22}{2} = \mathbf{11}$.

3.

* Solution by trying a simple operation: We begin by multiplying each side of the first equation by 5, and each side of the second equation by 12 to eliminate the denominators.

$$a + 3 = 100$$
$$a + b = 120$$

Now subtract the first equation from the second equation.

$$a + b = 120$$
$$\underline{a + 3 = 100}$$
$$b - 3 = 20$$

Finally, add 3 to each side of the resulting equation to get $b = \mathbf{23}$.

4.

* Solution by trying a simple operation: We divide each side of the equation by 7 to get $3x + 7y = \mathbf{4}$.

Note: When we divide the left hand side by 7, we have to divide **each** term by 7.

$$\frac{21x}{7} = 3x \qquad\qquad \frac{49y}{7} = 7y$$

Alternative: We can factor out 7 on the left hand side

$$21x + 49y = 7(3x + 7y).$$

So we have

$$21x + 49y = 28$$
$$7(3x + 7y) = 28$$
$$3x + 7y = 4.$$

5.

Solution by trying a simple operation: Let's rewrite the equations horizontally since that is how most of us are used to seeing equations.

$$5z + 4 + 4t + 8 + 9 = 52$$
$$2z + 4 + w + 8 + 9 = 34$$

116

We now use a simple operation. The operation to use here is subtraction. Let's go ahead and subtract term by term.

$$5z + 4 + 4t + 8 + 9 = 52$$
$$\underline{2z + 4 + w + 8 + 9 = 34}$$
$$3z + (4t - w) = 18$$

Remark: Whenever we are trying to find an expression that involves addition, subtraction, or both, **adding or subtracting** the given equations usually does the trick.

* Visualizing the answer: You can save a substantial amount of time by performing the subtraction in your head (left equation minus right equation). Note that above the lines the subtraction yields $3z + 4t - w$. This is exactly what we're looking for. Thus, we need only subtract below the lines to get the answer: $52 - 34 = \mathbf{18}$.

Solution by picking a number: If we choose any value for z, then t and w will be determined. So, let's set z equal to 0. Then

$$4 + 4t + 8 + 9 = 52$$
$$4t + 21 = 52$$
$$4t = 31$$
$$t = \frac{31}{4} = 7.75$$

and

$$4 + w + 8 + 9 = 34$$
$$w + 21 = 34$$
$$w = 13$$

So $3z + 4t - w = 0 + 4(7.75) - 13 = \mathbf{18}$.

Remarks: (1) Any choice for z will give us the same answer. We could have chosen a value for t or w as well. But once we choose a value for one of the variables the other two are determined.

(2) It was actually unnecessary to solve for t above. We could have stopped at $4t = 31$. We then have $3z + 4t - w = 0 + 31 - 13 = \mathbf{18}$.

    6.

* Solution by trying a simple operation: The operation to use here is multiplication.

$$ab = 4$$
$$bc = 1/3$$
$$(ab)(bc) = (4)(1/3)$$
$$ab^2c = 4/3$$

Now substitute 2 in for b^2. So we have $a(2)c = \frac{4}{3}$. Multiplying each side of the equation by $\frac{1}{2}$ gives us $ac = (\frac{4}{3})(\frac{1}{2}) = \mathbf{2/3}$.

Remarks: (1) Whenever we are trying to find an expression that involves multiplication, division, or both, **multiplying or dividing** the given equations usually does the trick.

(2) We could also grid in $.\mathbf{666}$ or $.\mathbf{667}$.

(3) If we had multiplied all 3 equations together we would have gotten $ab^4c = \frac{8}{3}$. This isn't as efficient, but it still works. Note that

$$b^4 = b^2b^2 = (2)(2) = 4. \text{ Thus, } ac = (\tfrac{8}{3})(\tfrac{1}{4}) = \mathbf{2/3}.$$

7.
* Solution by trying a simple operation: First multiply out the second term on the left hand side of the second equation: $ax + by + y = 35$. Now subtract the first equation from the second equation.

$$ax + by + y = 35$$
$$\underline{ax + by = 25}$$
$$y = 10$$

We see that the answer is choice (D).

8.
Solution by trying a simple operation: The operation to use here is multiplication.

$$xy = \ 6$$
$$yz = 10$$
$$\underline{xz = 15}$$
$$(xy)(yz)(xz) = (6)(10)(15)$$
$$x^2y^2z^2 = 900$$

Notice that we multiply all three left hand sides together, and all three right hand sides together. Now just take the square root of each side of the equation to get $xyz = 30$. Thus, the answer is **30**.

* Quick computation: With a little practice, we can get the solution to this type of problem very quickly. Here, we multiply the three numbers together to get $(6)(10)(15) = 900$. We then take the square root of 900 to get **30**.

9.

* Since we are trying to find x, we want to make y go away. So we make the two coefficients of y "match up" by multiplying by the appropriate numbers. We will multiply the first equation by 3 and the second equation by 4.

$$3(5x) = (1 + 4y)3$$
$$4(6x) = (2 - 3y)4$$

$$15x = 3 + 12y$$
$$24x = 8 - 12y$$

We now add the two equations.

$$15x = 3 + 12y$$
$$\underline{24x = 8 - 12y}$$
$$39x = 11$$

Now divide each side by 39 to get $x = \frac{11}{39}$. If we divide 11 by 39 in our calculator we get approximately $.28205128$. So we grid in $.\mathbf{282}$.

Remark: This method of solution is explained in more detail in the optional material at the end of this lesson.

10.

* Solution by trying a simple operation: The operation to use here is division. We divide the left hand sides of each equation, and the right hand sides of each equation. First the left. Recall that when we divide expressions with the same base we need to subtract the exponents. Therefore we have $\frac{x^{12}}{x^{11}} = x^1 = x$. For the right, recall that dividing is the same as multiplying by the reciprocal: $\left(\frac{3}{z}\right) \div \left(\frac{3y}{z}\right) = \left(\frac{3}{z}\right)\left(\frac{z}{3y}\right) = \frac{1}{y}$. Therefore, $x = \frac{1}{y}$ and the answer is choice (D).

Alternate Solution: Multiply each side of each equation by z to get

$$zx^{12} = 3$$
$$zx^{11} = 3y$$

Multiplying each side of the second equation by x yields

$$zx^{12} = 3xy$$

So we have $3xy = 3$ from which it follows that $xy = 1$, or equivalently $x = \frac{1}{y}$. Thus, the answer is choice (D).

OPTIONAL MATERIAL

Systems of Equations

There are several different ways to solve a system of equations. The most important method to know for the SAT is the **elimination method**. Let's start with a simple example.

$$x - y = 10$$
$$x + y = 40$$

The idea is to **eliminate** one of the variables. In this case we can easily eliminate y by adding the two equations.

$$
\begin{array}{r}
x - y = 10 \\
\underline{x + y = 40} \\
2x \quad\; = 50
\end{array}
$$

Thus, $x = 25$. If we also need to find y, we can simply substitute 25 in for x in either of the original equations. For example, substituting $x = 25$ into $x + y = 40$ yields $25 + y = 40$, or $y = 15$.

In general, to solve a system of equations using the elimination method follow these 3 steps.

(1) make sure the two equations are "lined up" properly.
(2) multiply each equation by a nonzero number in preparation for cancellation.
(3) add the two equations to eliminate one of the variables.

Let's look at a more sophisticated example.

$$2x = 7 - 3y$$
$$5y = 5 - 3x$$

First notice that the equations are not "lined up" properly. We fix this by adding $3y$ to each side of the first equation, and adding $3x$ to each side of the second equation.

$$2x + 3y = 7$$
$$3x + 5y = 5$$

We will now multiply each side of the first equation by 3, and each side of the second equation by -2.

$$3(2x + 3y) = (7)(3)$$
$$-2(3x + 5y) = (5)(-2)$$

Do not forget to distribute correctly on the left. Add the two equations.

$$6x + 9y = 21$$
$$\underline{-6x - 10y = -10}$$
$$-y = 11$$

So $y = -11$. We can now substitute $y = -11$ into say, the first equation to get $2x = 7 - 3(-11) = 7 + 33 = 40$, and so $x = 20$.

Remarks: (1) We could have also eliminated y first by multiplying the first equation by 5 and the second by -3 (or the first by -5 and the second by 3). In practice, if you are only looking for one variable, try to eliminate the one you are **not** looking for.

(2) I chose to multiply by a negative number so that we can add the equations instead of subtracting them. We could have also multiplied the first equation by 3, the second by 2, and subtracted the two equations, but a computational error is more likely to occur this way

Now you try one.

$$3x = 3 + 7y$$
$$2y = 5 - 5x$$

Answer: $x = 1$, $y = 0$

LESSON 14
GEOMETRY

Reminder: Before beginning this lesson remember to redo the problems from Lessons 2, 6 and 10 that you have marked off. Do not "unmark" a question unless you get it correct.

Figures are Drawn to Scale Unless Otherwise Stated

Try to answer the following question using this strategy. **Do not** check the solution until you have attempted this question yourself.

LEVEL 1: GEOMETRY

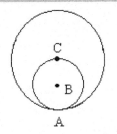

1. In the figure above, $A, B,$ and C lie on the same line. B is the center of the smaller circle, and C is the center of the larger circle. If the radius of the smaller circle is 7, what is the diameter of the larger circle?

* We can assume that the figure is drawn to scale.

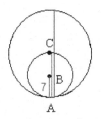

The three lines drawn in the picture above are just there for the purposes of measurement. In practice, you can just use your fingers to measure. The smallest segment is the radius of the smaller circle. The longest segment is the diameter of the larger circle. From the picture it is easy to see that the diameter of the larger circle is 4 times the radius of the smaller circle. So the answer is $(4)(7) = \mathbf{28}$.

Before we go on, try to give a complete geometric solution.

* Geometric solution: Since the diameter of a circle is twice the radius, the diameter of the smaller circle is $(2)(7) = 14$. This is also the radius of the larger circle. Therefore the diameter of the larger circle is $(2)(14) = \mathbf{28}$.

Draw Your Own Figure

Try to answer the following question using this strategy. **Do not** check the solution until you have attempted this question yourself.

LEVEL 2: GEOMETRY

2. C is the midpoint of line segment AB, and D and E are the midpoints of AC and CB, respectively. If the length of DE is 7, what is the length of AB?

    (A) 7
    (B) 10.5
    (C) 14
    (D) 17.5

* Let's draw a figure.

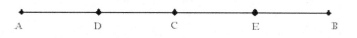

Since the length of DE is 7, the length of AD plus the length of EB is also 7. Therefore the length of AB is $7 + 7 = 14$, choice (C).

Parallel Lines Cut by a Transversal

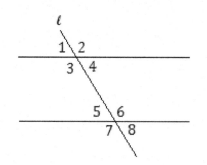

The figure above shows two parallel lines cut by the transversal ℓ.

123

Angles 1, 4, 5, and 8 all have the same measure. Also, angles 2, 3, 6, and 7 all have the same measure. Any two angles that do not have the same measure are supplementary, that is their measures add to 180°.

LEVEL 2: GEOMETRY

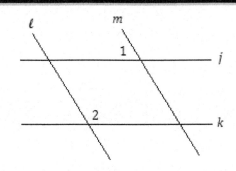

3. In the figure above, lines j and k are parallel and lines l and m are parallel. If the measure of ∠1 is 68°, what is the measure of ∠2 ?

(A) 158°
(B) 112°
(C) 98°
(D) 68°

* $m\angle 2 = 180° - m\angle 1 = 180° - 68° = 112°$, choice (B).

Similarity

Two triangles are **similar** if their angles are congruent. Note that similar triangles **do not** have to be the same size. Also note that to show that two triangles are similar we need only show that two pairs of angles are congruent. We get the third pair for free because all triangles have angle measures summing to 180 degrees.

Example:

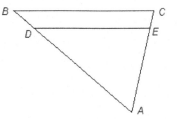

In the figure above, assume that $\overline{BC}$ is parallel to $\overline{DE}$. It then follows that angles ADE and ABC are congruent (corresponding angles). Since triangles ADE and ABC share angle A, the two triangles are similar.

Important Fact: Corresponding sides of similar triangles are in proportion.

So for example, in the figure above, $\frac{AD}{AB} = \frac{DE}{BC}$.

LEVEL 2: GEOMETRY

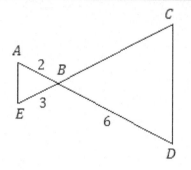

4.   In the figure above, $AE \parallel CD$ and segment AD intersects segment CE at B. What is the length of segment CE ?

* $\frac{BC}{BD} = \frac{BE}{BA}$. So $\frac{BC}{6} = \frac{3}{2}$. Thus, $2BC = 18$, and so $BC = \frac{18}{2} = 9$.

It follows that $CE = BC + BE = 9 + 3 = \mathbf{12}$.

You're doing great! Let's just practice a bit more. Try to solve each of the following problems by using one of the strategies you just learned. Then, if possible, solve each problem another way. The answers to these problems, followed by full solutions are at the end of this lesson. **Do not** look at the answers until you have attempted these problems yourself. Please remember to mark off any problems you get wrong.

LEVEL 1: GEOMETRY

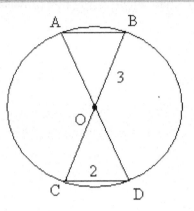

5. In the figure above, if O is the center of the circle, and AD and BC are diameters, which of the following statements is true?

    (A) $OC > 3$
    (B) $AB > 2$
    (C) $AB = 2$
    (D) $OA = 2$

LEVEL 2: GEOMETRY

6. What is the area of a right triangle whose sides have lengths 10, 24, and 26?

7. The sum of six adjacent nonoverlapping angles is 180 degrees. Five of the angles each have a measure of y degrees and the remaining angle measures 135 degrees. What is the value of y?

8. In the xy-plane, the point $(0,2)$ is the center of a circle that has radius 2. Which of the following is NOT a point on the circle?

    (A) $(0,4)$
    (B) $(-2,4)$
    (C) $(2,2)$
    (D) $(0,0)$

126

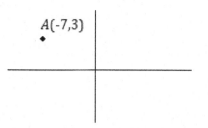

9. In the figure above, a line is to be drawn through point A so that it never crosses the x-axis. Through which of the following points must the line pass?

    (A) $(7,3)$
    (B) $(7,-3)$
    (C) $(-7,-3)$
    (D) $(3,7)$

LEVEL 3: GEOMETRY

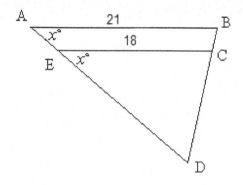

10. In the figure above, what is the value of $\frac{ED}{AD}$?

    (A) $\frac{1}{7}$

    (B) $\frac{1}{4}$

    (C) $\frac{1}{2}$

    (D) $\frac{6}{7}$

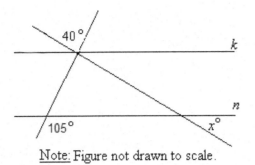

Note: Figure not drawn to scale.

11. In the figure above, $k \parallel n$. What is the value of x?

LEVEL 4: GEOMETRY

12. Point A is a vertex of a 6-sided polygon. The polygon has 6 sides of equal length and 6 angles of equal measure. When all possible diagonals are drawn from point A in the polygon, how many triangles are formed?

  (A) One
  (B) Two
  (C) Three
  (D) Four

Definitions Used in This Lesson

Definitions of a **triangle** and **circle** can be found on page 29. Definitions of a **linear pair** and **supplementary** can be found on page 91.

An **altitude** of a triangle is a straight line through a vertex of the triangle and perpendicular to a line containing the **base** opposite this vertex.

Two triangles are **similar** if their angles are congruent.

A **polygon** is a two-dimensional geometric figure formed of three or more straight sides. Some examples of polygons are triangles (3 sides), quadrilaterals (4 sides), pentagons (5 sides), hexagons (6 sides), heptagons (7 sides), and octagons (8 sides).

Formulas Used in This Lesson

The sum of the measures in degrees of the angles of a triangle is 180.

$d = 2r$ where d is the diameter of a circle, and r is the radius of the circle.

Area of a triangle: $A = \frac{1}{2}bh$ (in a right triangle the base and height are the two legs in either order).

The **hypotenuse** of a right triangle (the side opposite the right angle) is always longer than each **leg**.

Answers

1. 28	7. 9
2. C	8. B
3. B	9. A
4. 12	10. D
5. C	11. 65
6. 120	12. D

Full Solutions

5.

* Solution by assuming the figure is drawn to scale: It looks like AB and CD have the same length. So $AB = 2$ and the answer is choice (C).

Remark: It also looks like $OA = OB = OC = OD$, but there is no answer choice saying that any of these are equal to 3.

Geometric solution: Since OA, OB, OC and OD are all radii of the circle, they are equal in length. Thus, $OA = OB = OC = OD = 3$. The angles AOB and COD are **vertical angles** and are thus congruent. Minor arcs AB and CD have the same measure as angles AOB and COD, respectively since these two angles are central angles (**central angles have the same degree measure as their intercepted arcs**). Thus minor arcs AB and CD have the same measure. **If two minor arcs are equal in measure, their corresponding chords are equal in measure.** Therefore $AB = CD = 2$, choice (C).

6.

* Solution by drawing a picture:

129

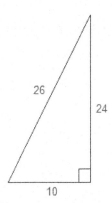

Remember: The **hypotenuse** of a right triangle (the side opposite the right angle) is always longer than both **legs**.

In a right triangle we can always take the two legs to be the base and the height (in either order). So $b = 10$, $h = 24$, and

$$A = \frac{1}{2}bh = \frac{1}{2}(10)(24) = \mathbf{120}.$$

7.

* Solution by drawing a picture: Let's begin by drawing a picture.

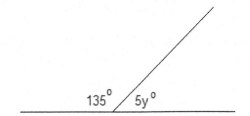

From the picture we see that $5y = 180 - 135 = 45$. So $y = \frac{45}{5} = \mathbf{9}$.

8.

* Solution by drawing a picture:

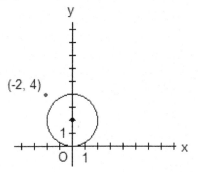

From the picture it should be clear that $(-2, 4)$ is not on the circle. This is choice (B).

9.

* Solution by drawing a picture: Let's draw the line.

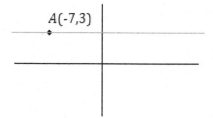

If the line never crosses the x-axis, then it is a horizontal line (as we can see from the picture). Therefore the y-coordinate of any point on the line is 3. Thus, the answer is choice (A).

10.

* Solution by assuming the figure is drawn to scale: Clearly ED is more than half the size of AD, so that $\frac{ED}{AD} > \frac{1}{2}$. Thus, the answer is $\frac{6}{7}$, choice (D).

Geometric solution: Triangles ECD and ABD are **similar**, and **corresponding sides of similar triangles are in proportion**. Therefore

$$\frac{ED}{AD} = \frac{EC}{AB} = \frac{18}{21} = \frac{6}{7}$$

Thus, the answer is choice (D).

Remarks: (1) To see that triangles ABD and ECD are similar, observe that BAD and CED are congruent, and the two triangles share angle D.

(2) When a triangle is inside another similar triangle it may help to draw the individual triangles next to each other, oriented so that congruent angles are in the same direction. See the figures below.

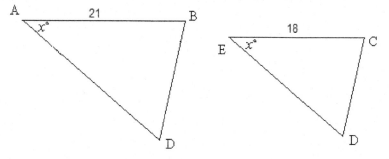

See the optional material below for another common example of this that is a bit more complicated.

11.

* We will use supplementary angles, vertical angles, and the fact that the angle measures of a triangle sum to 180° to find x.

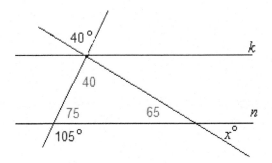

To clarify the picture above, $180 - 105 = 75$, the upper angle of the triangle has measure 40° because it is vertical with the other 40° angle, and $180 - 75 - 40 = 65$. Since the angle labeled by x is vertical with the 65 degree angle, $x = \mathbf{65}$.

12.

* **Solution by drawing a picture:**

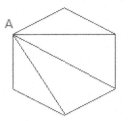

Observe that there are four triangles, choice (D).

OPTIONAL MATERIAL

Similarity in Right Triangles

Consider the following figure.

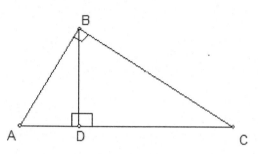

We have a right triangle with an **altitude** drawn from the right angle to the hypotenuse. In this figure triangles BDC, ADB, and ABC are similar to each other. When solving a problem involving this figure I strongly recommend redrawing all 3 triangles next to each other so that congruent angles match up. The 3 figures will look like this.

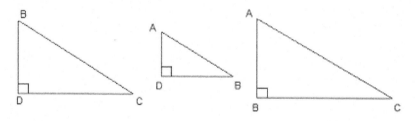

Let's look at two examples.

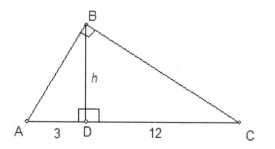

1. Solve for h in the triangle above.

Solution: We redraw the three triangles next to each other so that congruent angles match up.

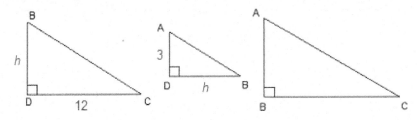

We now set up a ratio, cross multiply, and divide: $\frac{h}{12} = \frac{3}{h}$. So $h^2 = 36$, and therefore $h = 6$.

Remark: Clearly we didn't need to redraw the third triangle, but I suggest drawing all three until you get the hang of this.

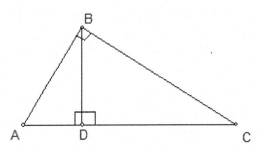

2. In the triangle above, $DC = 3$ and $BC = 6$. What is the value of AC ?

Solution: We redraw the three triangles next to each other so that congruent angles match up.

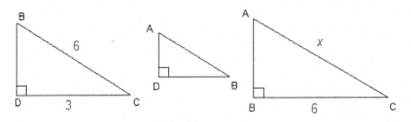

We now set up a ratio, cross multiply, and divide: $\frac{6}{3} = \frac{x}{6}$. So $36 = 3x$, and therefore $x = 12$.

Remark: Here we didn't actually need the second triangle.

LESSON 15
PASSPORT TO ADVANCED MATH

Reminder: Before beginning this lesson remember to redo the problems from Lessons 3, 7 and 11 that you have marked off. Do not "unmark" a question unless you get it correct.

Begin by quickly reviewing the following basic strategies:

<u>**Start with choice (B) or (C)**</u> – p. 15.
<u>**When NOT to start with choice (B) or (C)**</u> – p. 16.
<u>**Take a guess**</u> – p. 50.
<u>**Pick a number**</u> – p. 75.

Try to solve each of the following problems by using one of the four strategies above whenever you can. Then, if possible, solve each problem another way. The answers to these problems are at the end of this lesson. Please **do not** look at the answers until you have attempted each of these problems yourself. Remember to mark off any problems you get wrong.

LEVEL 1: ADVANCED MATH

1. If $3k^2 - 33 = 12 - 2k^2$, what are all possible values of k?

    (A) 3 only
    (B) −3 only
    (C) 0 only
    (D) 3 and −3 only

LEVEL 2: ADVANCED MATH

$$(a^3 - 3a^2b + 2ab^2 - b^3) - (-a^3 - 3a^2b - 2ab^2 - b^3)$$

2. Which of the following is equivalent to the expression above?

    (A) 0
    (B) $a^3 + b^3$
    (C) $-6a^2b - 2b^3$
    (D) $2a^3 + 4ab^2$

$$f(x) = |2x - 3| - 1$$

3.　For what positive value of x is $f(x)$ equal to 2 ?

　　(A) 0
　　(B) 2
　　(C) 3
　　(D) There is no such positive value of x.

$$4(5x + 1)(3x - 2)$$

4.　Which of the following is equivalent to the expression above?

　　(A) $60x^2 - 8$
　　(B) $60x^2 - 28x - 8$
　　(C) $12x^2 - 3$
　　(D) $20x$

LEVEL 3: ADVANCED MATH

$$7(a + b) = 2(b - a)$$

5.　If (a, b) is a solution to the equation above and $a \neq 0$, what is the ratio $\frac{b}{a}$?

　　(A) $-\frac{9}{5}$

　　(B) $-\frac{8}{5}$

　　(C) 8

　　(D) 11

6.　Jessica's car gets 18 miles per gallon when the car travels at an average speed of 35 miles per hour. Jessica begins a trip with 14 gallons of gas, and she travels at 35 miles per hour for the first 4 hours of her trip. Which of the following functions g is the most accurate model for the number of gallons of gas remaining in the tank t hours after the trip begins for $0 \leq t \leq 4$?

　　(A) $g(t) = \frac{14 - 35t}{18}$

　　(B) $g(t) = \frac{14 - 18t}{35}$

　　(C) $g(t) = 14 - \frac{35t}{18}$

　　(D) $g(t) = 14 - \frac{18}{35t}$

LEVEL 4: ADVANCED MATH

7.   Let the function f be defined for all values of x by $f(x) = x(x + 1)$. If k is a positive number and $f(k + 5) = 72$, what is the value of k?

8.   Let ⋔ be defined by $x ⋔ y = y^x$. If $a = x ⋔ 2$, $b = y ⋔ 2$, and $x + y = 3$, what is the value of ab ?

Answers

1. D	5. A
2. D	6. C
3. C	7. 3
4. B	8. 8

Download additional solutions for free here:

www.thesatmathprep.com/28Les500.html

LESSON 16
STATISTICS

Reminder: Before beginning this lesson remember to redo the problems from Lessons 4, 8 and 12 that you have marked off. Do not "unmark" a question unless you get it correct.

Turn to page 43 and review **Change averages to sums.** Then try to solve each of the following problems using this strategy whenever possible. The answers to these problems are at the end of this lesson. **Do not** look at the answers until you have attempted these problems yourself. If you are getting any of these questions wrong, go back and redo Lesson 4.

LEVEL 1: STATISTICS

1. The average (arithmetic mean) of four numbers is 50. If three of the numbers are 42, 52 and 62, what is the fourth number?

2. The average (arithmetic mean) of five numbers is 140. If the sum of four of the numbers is 541, what is the fifth number?

3. A biologist was interested in the number of times a field cricket chirps each minute on a sunny day. He randomly selected 100 field crickets from a garden, and found that the mean number of chirps per minute was 112, and the margin of error for this estimate was 6 chirps. The biologist would like to repeat the procedure and attempt to reduce the margin of error. Which of the following samples would most likely result in a smaller margin of error for the estimated mean number of times a field cricket chirps each minute on a sunny day?

   (A) 50 randomly selected crickets from the same garden.
   (B) 50 randomly selected field crickets from the same garden.
   (C) 200 randomly selected crickets from the same garden.
   (D) 200 randomly selected field crickets from the same garden.

138

LEVEL 2: STATISTICS

4. The average (arithmetic mean) of four numbers is 214. If one of the numbers is 67, what is the sum of the other three?

5. The average (arithmetic mean) of 7, 11, 15, and z is z. What is the value of z?

6. The average (arithmetic mean) of eleven numbers is 85. If a twelfth number, 37, is added to the group, what is the average of the twelve numbers?

7. For which of the following lists of 6 numbers is the mode NOT equal to the average (arithmetic mean)?

    (A) 2, 3, 3, 3, 3, 4
    (B) 2, 4, 4, 4, 5, 5
    (C) 3, 3, 3, 3, 5, 6
    (D) 4, 4, 5, 5, 5, 7

8. A is a set of numbers whose average (arithmetic mean) is 9. B is a set that is generated by multiplying each number in A by four. What is the average of the numbers in set B?

9. A psychologist wanted to determine if there is an association between diet and stress levels for the population of middle aged women in New York. He surveyed a random sample of 1500 middle aged female New Yorkers and found substantial evidence of a positive association between diet and stress levels. Which of the following conclusions is well supported by the data?

    (A) A dietary change causes an increase in stress levels for middle aged women from New York.
    (B) An increase in stress levels causes middle aged women from New York to change their diets.
    (C) There is a positive association between diet and stress levels for middle aged women in New York.
    (D) There is a positive association between diet and stress levels for middle aged women in the world.

LEVEL 3: STATISTICS

10. The average (arithmetic mean) of nine numbers is 30. When a tenth number is added, the average of the ten numbers is also 30. What is the tenth number?

11. The average of x, y, z, and w is 12 and the average of z and w is 7. What is the average of x and y?

12. The tables below give the distribution of the grades received by a class of 35 students on a math exam and a chemistry exam.

Math Exam			Chemistry Exam	
Grade	Frequency		Grade	Frequency
100	7		100	1
95	5		95	4
90	5		90	26
85	4		85	2
80	6		80	1
75	8		75	1

Which of the following is true about the data shown for these 35 students?

(A) The standard deviation of grades on the math exam is larger.
(B) The standard deviation of grades on the chemistry exam is larger.
(C) The standard deviation of grades on the math exam is the same as that of the chemistry exam.
(D) The standard deviation of grades on these two exams cannot be calculated with the data provided.

LEVEL 4: STATISTICS

13. If the average (arithmetic mean) of k and $k + 3$ is b and if the average of k and $k - 3$ is c, what is the average of b and c?

(A) 1
(B) $\frac{k}{2}$
(C) k
(D) $k + \frac{1}{2}$

14. The average (arithmetic mean) age of the people in a certain group was 20 years before one of the members left the group and was replaced by someone who is 6 years older than the person who left. If the average age of the group is now 22 years, how many people are in the group?

15. The average (arithmetic mean) of 4 numbers is m. If one of the numbers is n, what is the average of the remaining 3 numbers in terms of m and n?

   (A) $\frac{m}{4}$

   (B) $4m + n$

   (C) $\frac{3m-n}{4}$

   (D) $\frac{4m-n}{3}$

Definitions Used in This Lesson

Definitions of **average (arithmetic mean)**, and **median** can be found on pages 45 and 46.

The **mode** of a set of numbers is the number that occurs most frequently. There can be more than one mode if more than one number occurs with the greatest frequency.

The **standard deviation** of a set of numbers measures how far the numbers are from the arithmetic mean.

Answers

1. 44	4. 789	7. C	10. 30	13. C
2. 159	5. 11	8. 36	11. 17	14. 3
3. D	6. 81	9. C	12. A	15. D

OPTIONAL MATERIAL

CHALLENGE QUESTION: STATISTICS

Let $x_1, x_2, \ldots, x_n$ be a list of numbers with average a. Show that the average of $x_1, x_2, \ldots, x_n, a$ is also a.

Solution to Challenge Question

We will use the strategy of changing averages to sums. For the original list, the Average is a and the Number is n. It follows that the Sum is $x_1 + x_2 + \cdots + x_n = an$. Add a to each side of this equation to get $x_1 + x_2 + \cdots + x_n + a = an + a$. Then factor a on the right to get $x_1 + x_2 + \cdots + x_n + a = a(n + 1)$. Finally divide by $n + 1$, and we have $\frac{x_1 + x_2 + \cdots + x_n + a}{n+1} = a$.

The left hand side of this last equation is precisely the average of the new list of numbers, and we have shown that this average is equal to a.

Download additional solutions for free here:

www.thesatmathprep.com/28Les500.html

LESSON 17
COMPLEX NUMBERS

Reminder: Before beginning this lesson remember to redo the problems from Lessons 1, 5, 9 and 13 that you have marked off. Do not "unmark" a question unless you get it correct.

Complex Numbers

A **complex number** has the form $a + bi$ where a and b are real numbers and $i = \sqrt{-1}$.

Example: The following are complex numbers:

$$2 + 3i \quad \frac{3}{2} + (-2i) = \frac{3}{2} - 2i \quad -\pi + 2.6i \quad \sqrt{-9} = 3i$$

$0 + 5i = 5i$ This is called a **pure imaginary** number.

$17 + 0i = 17$ This is called a **real number.**

$0 + 0i = 0$ This is **zero.**

Addition and subtraction: We add two complex numbers simply by adding their real parts, and then adding their imaginary parts.

$$(a + bi) + (c + di) = (a + c) + (b + d)i$$

LEVEL 1: COMPLEX NUMBERS

1. For $i = \sqrt{-1}$, the sum $(1 + 2i) + (3 - 4i)$ is

    (A) $4 + 6i$
    (B) $4 - 2i$
    (C) $2 + 6i$
    (D) $2 - 2i$

* $(1 + 2i) + (3 - 4i) = (1 + 3) + (2 - 4)i = 4 - 2i$, choice (B).

Multiplication: We can multiply two complex numbers by formally taking the product of two binomials and then replacing i^2 by -1.

$$(a + bi)(c + di) = (ac - bd) + (ad + bc)i$$

143

LEVEL 3: COMPLEX NUMBERS

2. Which of the following complex numbers is equivalent to $(1 + 2i)(3 - 4i)$? (Note: $i = \sqrt{-1}$)

    (A) $3 - 8i$
    (B) $4 - 2i$
    (C) $11 + 2i$
    (D) $11 - 2i$

* $(1 + 2i)(3 - 4i) = (3 + 8) + (-4 + 6)i = 11 + 2i$, choice (C).

The **conjugate** of the complex number $a + bi$ is the complex number $a - bi$.

Example: The conjugate of $-5 + 6i$ is $-5 - 6i$.

Note that when we multiply conjugates together we always get a real number. In fact, we have

$$(a + bi)(a - bi) = a^2 + b^2$$

Division: We can put the quotient of two complex numbers into standard form by multiplying both the numerator and denominator by the conjugate of the denominator. This is best understood with an example.

LEVEL 4: COMPLEX NUMBERS

$$\frac{1 + 5i}{2 - 3i}$$

3. If the expression above is rewritten in the form $a + bi$, where a and b are real numbers, what is the value of $b - a$?

* We multiply the numerator and denominator of $\frac{1+5i}{2-3i}$ by $(2 + 3i)$ to get

$$\frac{(1+5i)}{(2-3i)} \cdot \frac{(2+3i)}{(2+3i)} = \frac{(2-15)+(3+10)i}{4+9} = \frac{-13+13i}{13} = -\frac{13}{13} + \frac{13}{13}i = -1 + i$$

So $a = -1$, $b = 1$, and $b - a = 1 - (-1) = 1 + 1 = \mathbf{2}$.

Now try to solve each of the following problems. The answers to these problems, followed by full solutions are at the end of this lesson. **Do not** look at the answers until you have attempted these problems yourself. Please remember to mark off any problems you get wrong.

LEVEL 1: COMPLEX NUMBERS

4. If $(-5 + 2i) + (-1 - 3i) = a + bi$ and $i = \sqrt{-1}$, then what is the value of ab ?

LEVEL 2: COMPLEX NUMBERS

5. When we subtract $2 - 3i$ from $-5 + 6i$ we get which of the following complex numbers?

   (A) $-7 + 3i$
   (B) $-7 + 9i$
   (C) $-3 - 3i$
   (D) $-3 + 3i$

LEVEL 4: COMPLEX NUMBERS

6. * If $i = \sqrt{-1}$, and $\frac{(3+4i)}{(-5-2i)} = a + bi$, where a and b are real numbers, then what is the value of $|b|$ to the nearest tenth?

7. If u and v are real numbers, $i = \sqrt{-1}$, and

$$(u - v) + 3i = 7 + vi,$$

   then what is $u + v$?

8. If $(x - 3i)(5 + yi) = 28 - 3i$ then what is one possible value of $x + y$? (Note: $i = \sqrt{-1}$)

Answers

1. B	5. B
2. C	6. 5
3. 2	7. D
4. 6	8. 8

145

Full Solutions

4.

* $(-5 + 2i) + (-1 - 3i) = (-5 - 1) + (2 - 3)i = -6 - i$. So $a = -6$, $b = -1$, and therefore $ab = (-6)(-1) = \mathbf{6}$.

5.

* $(-5 + 6i) - (2 - 3i) = -5 + 6i - 2 + 3i = -7 + 9i$, choice (B).

6.

* $\dfrac{(3+4i)}{(-5-2i)} = \dfrac{(3+4i)}{(-5-2i)} \cdot \dfrac{(-5+2i)}{(-5+2i)} = \dfrac{(-15-8)+(6-20)i}{25+4} = \dfrac{-23-14i}{29} = -\dfrac{23}{29} - \dfrac{14}{29}i$

So $b = -\dfrac{14}{29}$.

Therefore $|b| = \dfrac{14}{29} \approx .4827586207$. To the nearest tenth this is $.\mathbf{5}$.

7.

* Two complex numbers are equal if their real parts are equal and their imaginary parts are equal. So we have

$$u - v = 7 \qquad \text{and} \qquad 3 = v.$$

Since $v = 3$ (from the second equation), we have that $u - 3 = 7$. Thus, $u = 7 + 3 = 10$. Finally, $u + v = 10 + 3 = \mathbf{13}$.

8.

* $(x - 3i)(5 + yi) = (5x + 3y) + (-15 + xy)i$. So $5x + 3y = 28$ and $-15 + xy = -3$. So $xy = 12$. We need to solve the following system of equations:

$$5x + 3y = 28$$
$$xy = 12$$

There are several ways to solve this formally, but we can also just try guessing. We are looking for two numbers that multiply to 12. If we try $x = 2, y = 6$, we see that $5x + 3y = 5(2) + 3(6) = 10 + 18 = 28$.

So a possible solution to the system is $x = 2$, $y = 6$, and in this case $x + y = \mathbf{8}$.

OPTIONAL MATERIAL

Solving Systems of Equations with Your Calculator

In the optional material from Lesson 13 we went over how to solve a small system of equations using the elimination method. Here I will show you how to solve the same systems using your calculator. As usual I assume you are using a TI-84 calculator or something equivalent. Let's look at this simple example.

$$x - y = 10$$
$$x + y = 40$$

Begin by pushing the MATRIX button (which is 2ND x^{-1}). Scroll over to EDIT and then select [A] (or press 1). We will be inputting a 2×3 matrix, so press 2 ENTER 3 ENTER. We then begin entering the numbers 1, -1, and 10 for the first row, and 1, 1, and 40 for the second row. To do this we can simply type 1 ENTER -1 ENTER 10 ENTER 1 ENTER 1 ENTER 40 ENTER.

Note: What we have just done was create the **augmented matrix** for the system of equations. This is simply an array of numbers which contains the coefficients of the variables together with the right hand sides of the equations.

Now push the QUIT button (2ND MODE) to get a blank screen. Press MATRIX again. This time scroll over to MATH and select rref((or press B). Then press MATRIX again and select [A] (or press 1) and press ENTER.

Note: What we have just done is put the matrix into **reduced row echelon form**. In this form we can read off the solution to the original system of equations.

Warning: Be careful to use the rref(button (2 r's), and not the ref button (which has only one r).

Your display will show the following.

$$[\,[1\ 0\ 25]$$
$$[0\ 1\ 15]\,]$$

The first line is interpreted as $x = 25$ and the second line as $y = 15$.

Let's look at a more sophisticated example.

$$2x = 7 - 3y$$
$$5y = 5 - 3x$$

First notice that the equations are not "lined up" properly. We fix this by adding $3y$ to each side of the first equation, and adding $3x$ to each side of the second equation.

$$2x + 3y = 7$$
$$3x + 5y = 5$$

Now we press MATRIX, scroll over to EDIT, select [A], input 2 ENTER 3 ENTER followed by 2 ENTER 3 ENTER 7 ENTER 3 ENTER 5 ENTER 5 ENTER. We then push QUIT followed by MATRIX, we scroll over to MATH and select rref(. We press MATRIX again, select [A] and press ENTER. We get the following.

$$[[1\ 0\ 20]$$
$$[0\ 1 - 11]]$$

In other words, $x = 20$ and $y = -11$

Now you try this one yourself.

$$3x = 3 + 7y$$
$$2y = 5 - 5x$$

Answer: $x = 1, y = 0$

Notes: (1) Make sure that all the variables are on the left hand sides of the equations, the constants are on the right hand sides of the equations, and the variables are all lined up correctly (first column x's, second column y's).

(2) This procedure is known in higher mathematics as **Gauss-Jordan Reduction**.

This method works equally well on larger systems of equations. Try to solve the following system using your calculator.

$$2x + 3y - 4z = 2$$
$$x - y + 5z = 6$$
$$3x + 2y - z = 4$$

Answer: $x = -.4, y = 3.6, z = 2$

148

LESSON 18
GEOMETRY AND TRIGONOMETRY

Reminder: Before beginning this lesson remember to redo the problems from Lessons 2, 6, 10 and 14 that you have marked off. Do not "unmark" a question unless you get it correct.

The Pythagorean Theorem

The Pythagorean Theorem says that if a right triangle has legs of length a and b, and a hypotenuse of length c, then $c^2 = a^2 + b^2$. Note that the Pythagorean Theorem is one of the formulas given to you in the beginning of each math section.

Try to answer the following question using the Pythagorean Theorem. **Do not** check the solution until you have attempted this question yourself.

LEVEL 3: GEOMETRY

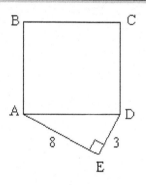

1.   In the figure above, what is the area of square $ABCD$?

* Let x be the length of a side of the square. So $AD = x$. We now use the Pythagorean Theorem.

$$x^2 = 8^2 + 3^2 = 64 + 9 = 73.$$

But x^2 is precisely the area of the square. Therefore the answer is **73**.

149

Right Triangle Trigonometry

Let's consider the following right triangle, and let's focus our attention on angle A.

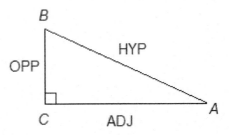

Note that the **hypotenuse** is ALWAYS the side opposite the right angle.

The other two sides of the right triangle, called the **legs**, depend on which angle is chosen. In this picture we chose to focus on angle A. Therefore the opposite side is BC, and the adjacent side is AC.

It's worth memorizing how to compute the three basic trig functions:

$$\sin A = \frac{\text{OPP}}{\text{HYP}} \qquad \cos A = \frac{\text{ADJ}}{\text{HYP}} \qquad \tan A = \frac{\text{OPP}}{\text{ADJ}}$$

Here is a tip to help you remember these:

Many students find it helpful to use the word SOHCAHTOA. You can think of the letters here as representing sin, opp, hyp, cos, adj, hyp, tan, opp, adj.

Example: Compute the three basic trig functions for each of the angles (except the right angle) in the triangle below.

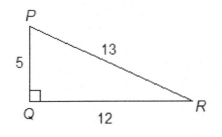

Solution:

$$\sin P = \frac{12}{13} \qquad \cos P = \frac{5}{13} \qquad \tan P = \frac{12}{5}$$

$$\sin R = \frac{5}{13} \qquad \cos R = \frac{12}{13} \qquad \tan R = \frac{5}{12}$$

150

LEVEL 2: TRIGONOMETRY

2. If $0 \leq x \leq 90°$ and $\cos x = \frac{5}{13}$, then $\tan x =$

* Trigonometric solution: Let's draw a picture. We begin with a right triangle and label one of the angles x.

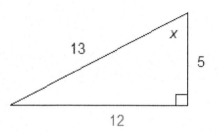

Since $\cos x = \frac{\text{ADJ}}{\text{HYP}}$, we label the leg adjacent to x with a 5 and the hypotenuse with 13. We can use the Pythagorean triple 5, 12, 13 to see that the other side is 12.

Finally, $\tan x = \frac{\text{OPP}}{\text{ADJ}} = \mathbf{12/5}$ or $\mathbf{2.4}$.

Notes: (1) The most common Pythagorean triples are 3, 4, 5 and 5, 12, 13. Two others that may come up are 8, 15, 17 and 7, 24, 25.

(2) If you don't remember the Pythagorean triple 5, 12, 13, you can use the Pythagorean Theorem:

Here we have $5^2 + b^2 = 13^2$. Therefore $25 + b^2 = 169$. Subtracting 25 from each side of this equation gives $b^2 = 169 - 25 = 144$. So $b = 12$.

(3) The equation $b^2 = 144$ would normally have two solutions: $b = 12$ and $b = -12$. But the length of a side of a triangle cannot be negative, so we reject -12.

Special Right Triangles

Recall that the following two special right triangles are given to you on the SAT.

151

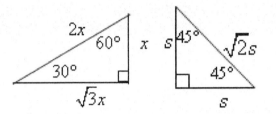

Now try to answer the following question. **Do not** check the solution until you have attempted this question yourself.

LEVEL 4: TRIGONOMETRY

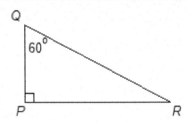

3. In the triangle above, $QR = 8$. What is the area of $\triangle PQR$?

  (A) $32\sqrt{3}$
  (B) 32
  (C) $16\sqrt{3}$
  (D) $8\sqrt{3}$

* Solution using a 30, 60, 90 triangle: Using the special 30, 60, 90 triangle we can label each side with its length as follows.

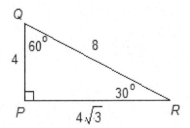

The area is then $A = \frac{1}{2}bh = \frac{1}{2}(4\sqrt{3})(4) = 8\sqrt{3}$, choice (D).

Note: The hypotenuse of a 30, 60, 90 triangle is always twice the length of the side opposite the 30 degree angle.

Also, if we always think of a side as going with its opposite angle, there will never be any confusion, even if our picture is facing a different direction than the triangle on the SAT. This is actually good advice for any triangle problem. Always think of a side in terms of its opposite angle and vice versa.

Trigonometric solution: Let's label the sides of the triangle.

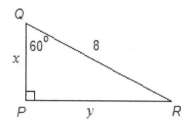

We have $\cos 60° = \frac{\text{ADJ}}{\text{HYP}} = \frac{x}{8}$. So $x = 8 \cos 60°$.

We also have $\sin 60° = \frac{\text{OPP}}{\text{HYP}} = \frac{y}{8}$. So $y = 8 \sin 60°$.

The area of the triangle is

$$\frac{1}{2}xy = \frac{1}{2} \cdot 8 \cos 60° \cdot 8 \sin 60° = 32 \cdot \frac{1}{2} \cdot \frac{\sqrt{3}}{2} = 8\sqrt{3}$$

This is choice (D).

Notes: (1) If we are allowed to use a calculator for this problem we could do the computation $\frac{1}{2} \cdot 8 \cos 60° \cdot 8 \sin 60°$ right in our calculator to get approximately 13.8564.

We could then put the answer choices in our calculator to see which choice matches that decimal approximation. We see $8\sqrt{3} \approx 13.8564$. So the answer is choice (D).

(2) We could use the special 30, 60, 90 triangle to get

$$\cos 60° = \frac{\text{ADJ}}{\text{HYP}} = \frac{1}{2} \quad \text{and} \quad \sin 60° = \frac{\text{OPP}}{\text{HYP}} = \frac{\sqrt{3}}{2}$$

So we have $\frac{1}{2} \cdot 8 \cos 60° \cdot 8 \sin 60° = \frac{1}{2} \cdot 8 \cdot \frac{1}{2} \cdot 8 \cdot \frac{\sqrt{3}}{2} = 8\sqrt{3}$, choice (D).

(3) We can actually substitute any value for x in the picture of the 30, 60, 90 triangle that we like, because the x's always cancel when doing any trigonometric computation. For example, with $x = 1$, we have the following picture:

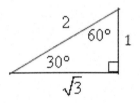

You're doing great! Let's just practice a bit more. Try to solve each of the following problems. The answers to these problems, followed by full solutions are at the end of this lesson. **Do not** look at the answers until you have attempted these problems yourself. Please remember to mark off any problems you get wrong.

LEVEL 1: GEOMETRY AND TRIG

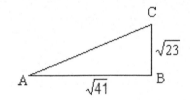

Note: Figure not drawn to scale.

4.   In right triangle ABC above, what is the length of side AC ?

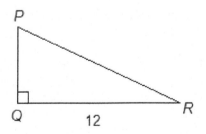

5.   In $\triangle PQR$ above, $\tan R = \frac{5}{12}$. What is the length of side PR ?

LEVEL 3: GEOMETRY

6. In a right triangle, one angle measures $x°$, where $\sin x° = \frac{3}{5}$. What is $\cos((90 - x)°)$?

LEVEL 4: GEOMETRY

7. What is the area of a square whose diagonal has length $6\sqrt{2}$?

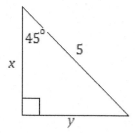

8. * In the triangle above, what is the value of $2x + y$ to the nearest tenth?

Definitions Used in This Lesson

Definitions of **perfect squares**, **triangles**, **quadrilaterals**, **rectangles**, and **squares** can be found on page 29.

Formulas Used in This Lesson

The sum of the measures in degrees of the angles of a triangle is 180.

Perimeter of a rectangle is $P = 2l + 2w$

Area of a square is $A = s^2$ or $A = \frac{d^2}{2}$

Answers

1. 73
2. 12/5 or 2.4
3. D
4. 8

5. 13
6. 3/5 or .6
7. 36
8. 10.6

Full Solutions

4.

* We use the Pythagorean Theorem: $c^2 = a^2 + b^2 = 23 + 41 = 64$. Therefore $AC = c = \mathbf{8}$.

5.

* Since $\tan R = \dfrac{\text{OPP}}{\text{ADJ}}$, we have $\dfrac{5}{12} = \dfrac{\text{OPP}}{\text{ADJ}}$. Since the adjacent side is 12, the opposite side must be 5. So we have the following picture.

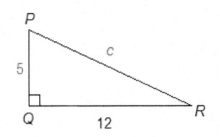

We now find PR by using the Pythagorean Theorem, or better yet, recognizing the Pythagorean triple 5, 12, 13.

So $PR = \mathbf{13}$.

Remarks: (1) If you don't remember the Pythagorean triple 5, 12, 13, you can use the Pythagorean Theorem.

In this problem we have $c^2 = 5^2 + 12^2 = 169$. So $c = 13$.

(2) See problem 2 for more information about Pythagorean triples and the Pythagorean Theorem.

(3) The equation $c^2 = 169$ would normally have two solutions: $c = 13$ and $c = -13$. But the length of a side of a triangle cannot be negative, so we reject -13.

6.

Basic trig solution: Let's draw a picture:

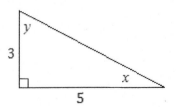

Notice that I labeled one of the angles with x, and used the fact that $\sin x = \frac{\text{OPP}}{\text{HYP}}$ to label 2 sides of the triangle.

Now observe that $y° = (90 - x)°$, so that

$$\cos((90 - x)°) = \cos y° = \frac{\text{ADJ}}{\text{HYP}} = \mathbf{3/5} \text{ or } \mathbf{.6}.$$

* Solution using a cofunction identity: $\cos((90 - x)°) = \sin x° = \mathbf{3/5}.$

Note: See the Optional Material below for the identity used here.

7.
We begin by drawing a picture

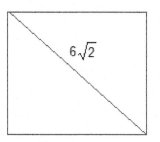

Solution using the Pythagorean Theorem: Since all sides of a square have equal length, an isosceles right triangle is formed. If we let x be the length of a side of the square, then by the Pythagorean Theorem

$$x^2 + x^2 = \left(6\sqrt{2}\right)^2$$
$$2x^2 = 72$$
$$x^2 = 36$$
$$x = 6$$

Thus, the area of the square is $(6)(6) = \mathbf{36}$.

Remark: We did a bit more work than we had to here. The area of the square is $A = x^2$. We already found that $x^2 = 36$. There was no need to solve this equation for x.

Solution using a 45, 45, 90 triangle: An isosceles right triangle is the same as a 45, 45, 90 triangle. So we can get the length of a side of the triangle just by looking at the formula in the front of any math section of the SAT. Here s is 6. The area of the square is then $(6)(6) = \mathbf{36}$.

* Using an area formula: The area of a square is $A = \frac{d^2}{2}$ where d is the length of the diagonal of the square. Therefore in this problem

$$A = \frac{d^2}{2} = \frac{\left(6\sqrt{2}\right)^2}{2} = \frac{72}{2} = 36.$$

8.

Solution using the Pythagorean Theorem: Since two of the angles have equal measure (they both measure 45 degrees), the triangle is isosceles, and we see that $x = y$. By the Pythagorean Theorem

$$x^2 + x^2 = 5^2$$
$$2x^2 = 25$$
$$x^2 = \frac{25}{2}$$
$$x = \frac{5}{\sqrt{2}}$$

Therefore $2x + y = 2x + x = 3x = \frac{15}{\sqrt{2}} \approx 10.6066$. So we grid in **10.6**.

* Solution using special triangles: Note that this is a 45, 45, 90 right triangle. Using the special triangle given at the beginning of each math section of the SAT we see that x and y are both equal to s, and $s\sqrt{2} = 5$. Therefore $s = \frac{5}{\sqrt{2}}$ and $2x + y = 2s + s = 3s = \frac{15}{\sqrt{2}} \approx 10.6066$. So we grid in **10.6**.

OPTIONAL MATERIAL

Trigonometric Identities

Quotient Identity: $\tan x = \frac{\sin x}{\cos x}$

Negative Identities:

$\cos(-x) = \cos x \qquad \sin(-x) = -\sin x \qquad \tan(-x) = -\tan x$

Cofunction Identities:

$\sin(90° - x) = \cos x \qquad\qquad \cos(90° - x) = \sin x$

Pythagorean Identity: $\cos^2 x + \sin^2 x = 1$

LESSON 19
PASSPORT TO ADVANCED MATH

Reminder: Before beginning this lesson remember to redo the problems from Lessons 3, 7, 11 and 15 that you have marked off. Do not "unmark" a question unless you get it correct.

Factoring

Recall from Lesson 7 that the **distributive property** says that for all real numbers a, b, and c, $a(b + c) = ab + ac$

When we use the distributive property in the opposite direction, we usually call it **factoring**: $ab + ac = a(b + c)$

Here are some more sophisticated techniques for factoring:

The Difference of Two Squares: $a^2 - b^2 = (a - b)(a + b)$

Examples: (1) $x^2 - 9 = (x - 3)(x + 3)$

(2) $4x^2 - 25y^2 = (2x - 5y)(2x + 5y)$

(3) $36 - 49x^2y^2 = (6 - 7xy)(6 + 7xy)$

Trinomial Factoring: $x^2 - (a + b)x + ab = (x - a)(x - b)$

Examples: (1) $x^2 - 5x + 6 = (x - 2)(x - 3)$

(2) $x^2 - 2x - 35 = (x - 7)(x + 5)$

(3) $x^2 + 14x + 33 = (x + 3)(x + 11)$

LEVEL 3: ADVANCED MATH

$$16b^2 - 4a^2$$

1. Which of the following is equivalent to the expression above?

(A) $(4b - 2a)^2$
(B) $(4b + 2a)^2$
(C) $(b - a)(16b + 4a)$
(D) $(4b - 2a)(4b + 2a)$

* Solution using the difference of two squares:

$$16b^2 - 4a^2 = (4b - 2a)(4b + 2a), \text{ choice (D).}$$

Notes: (1) The positive square root of $16b^2$ is $4b$, and the positive square root of $4a^2$ is $2a$.

(2) This problem can also be solved by picking numbers. I leave this solution to the reader.

Square Root Property

The **square root property** says that if $x^2 = a^2$, then $x = \pm a$.

For example, the equation $x^2 = 9$ has the two solutions $x = 3$ and $x = -3$.

Important note: Using the square root property is different from taking a square root. We apply the square root property to an equation of the form $x^2 = a^2$ to get two solutions, whereas when we take the positive square root of a number we get just one answer.

For example when we take the positive square root of 9 we get 3, i.e. $\sqrt{9} = 3$. But when we apply the square root property to the equation $x^2 = 9$, we have seen that we get the two solutions $x = 3$ and $x = -3$.

LEVEL 3: ADVANCED MATH

$$(x - 3)^2 = 2$$

2.   What is the solution set of the above equation?

(A) $\{1, 5\}$
(B) $\{3 + \sqrt{2}\}$
(C) $\{3 - \sqrt{2}, 3 + \sqrt{2}\}$
(D) The equation has no solutions.

* Solution using the square root property: When we apply the square root property we get $x - 3 = \pm\sqrt{2}$. We then add 3 to each side of this last equation to get the two solutions $x = 3 \pm \sqrt{2}$, choice (C).

Completing the Square

Completing the square is a technique with many useful applications. We complete the square on an expression of the form

$$x^2 + bx$$

To complete the square we simply take half of b, and then square the result. In other words we get $\left(\frac{b}{2}\right)^2$.

The expression $x^2 + bx + \left(\frac{b}{2}\right)^2$ is always a perfect square. In fact,

$$x^2 + bx + \left(\frac{b}{2}\right)^2 = \left(x + \frac{b}{2}\right)^2$$

For example, let's complete the square in the expression $x^2 + 6x$.

Well half of 6 is 3, and when we square 3 we get 9. So the new expression is $x^2 + 6x + 9$ which factors as $(x + 3)^2$.

Important notes: (1) When we complete the square we usually get an expression that is <u>not</u> equal to the original expression. For example, $x^2 + 6x \neq x^2 + 6x + 9$.

(2) The coefficient of x^2 <u>must</u> be 1 before we complete the square. So, for example, we cannot complete the square on the expression $2x^2 + 32x$.

But we can first factor out the 2 to get $2(x^2 + 16x)$, and then complete the square on the expression $x^2 + 16x$ to get $2(x^2 + 16x + 64)$.

Note that we increased the expression by $2 \cdot 64 = 128$.

We will see applications of completing the square below.

Solving Quadratic Equations

A quadratic equation has the form $\boldsymbol{ax^2 + bx + c = 0}$.

Let's use a simple example to illustrate the various methods for solving such an equation

LEVEL 3: ADVANCED MATH

$$x^2 - 2x = 15$$

3.   In the quadratic equation above, find the positive solution for x.

Solution by guessing: We plug in guesses for x until we find the answer. For example, if we guess that $x = 3$, then we get $3^2 - 2 \cdot 3 = 9 - 6 = 3$. This is too small.

Let's try $x = 5$ next. We get $5^2 - 2 \cdot 5 = 25 - 10 = 15$. This is correct. So the answer is **5**.

Solution by factoring: We bring everything to the left hand side of the equation to get $x^2 - 2x - 15 = 0$. We then factor the left hand side to get $(x - 5)(x + 3) = 0$. So $x - 5 = 0$ or $x + 3 = 0$. It follows that $x = 5$ or $x = -3$. Since we want the positive solution for x, the answer is **5**.

Solution by using the quadratic formula: As in the last solution we bring everything to the left hand side of the equation to get

$$x^2 - 2x - 15 = 0.$$

We identify $a = 1$, $b = -2$, and $c = -15$.

$$x = \frac{-b \pm \sqrt{b^2 - 4ac}}{2a} = \frac{2 \pm \sqrt{4 + 60}}{2} = \frac{2 \pm \sqrt{64}}{2} = \frac{2 \pm 8}{2} = 1 \pm 4.$$

So we get $x = 1 + 4 = 5$ or $x = 1 - 4 = -3$. Since we want the positive solution for x, the answer is **5**.

Solution by completing the square: For this solution we leave the constant on the right hand side: $x^2 - 2x = 15$.

We take half of -2, which is -1, and square this number to get 1. We then add 1 to each side of the equation to get $x^2 - 2x + 1 = 15 + 1$. This is equivalent to $(x - 1)^2 = 16$. We now apply the square root property to get $x - 1 = \pm 4$. So $x = 1 \pm 4$. This yields the two solutions $1 + 4 = 5$, and $1 - 4 = -3$. Since we want the positive solution for x, the answer is **5**.

Graphical solution: In your graphing calculator press the Y= button, and enter the following.

$$Y1 = X^2 - 2X - 15$$

Now press ZOOM 6 to graph the parabola in a standard window. Then press 2nd TRACE (which is CALC) 2 (or select ZERO), move the cursor just to the left of the second x-intercept and press ENTER. Now move the cursor just to the right of the second x-intercept and press ENTER again. Press ENTER once more, and you will see that the x-coordinate of the second x-intercept is **5**.

Now try to solve each of the following problems. The answers to these problems, followed by full solutions are at the end of this lesson. **Do not** look at the answers until you have attempted these problems yourself. Please remember to mark off any problems you get wrong.

LEVEL 2: ADVANCED MATH

4. The expression $x^2 + 2x - 35$ can be written as the product of two binomial factors with integer coefficients. One of the binomials is $(x + 7)$. If the other binomial is $(x - b)$, what is the value of b ?

LEVEL 3: ADVANCED MATH

$$16x^6 + 40x^3y^2 + 25y^4$$

5. Which of the following is equivalent to the expression above?

(A) $(4x^3 + 5y^2)^2$
(B) $(4x^2 + 5y)^4$
(C) $(16x^3 + 25y^2)^2$
(D) $(16x^2 + 25y)^4$

6. In the xy-plane, the parabola with equation $y = (x - 3)^2$ intersects the line with equation $y = 4$ at two points, P and Q. What is the length of $\overline{PQ}$?

LEVEL 4: ADVANCED MATH

$$h(x) = x^2 + 4x - 21$$

7. Which of the following is an equivalent form of the function h above in which the x-intercepts appear as constants or coefficients?

(A) $h(x) = (x - (-3))(x - 7)$
(B) $h(x) = (x - 3)(x - (-7))$
(C) $h(x) = (x - 2)^2 - 21$
(D) $h(x) = (x + 2)^2 - 25$

LEVEL 5: ADVANCED MATH

8. What are the solutions to $5x^2 - 30x + 20 = 0$?

163

(A) $x = -20 \pm 20\sqrt{5}$
(B) $x = -20 \pm \sqrt{5}$
(C) $x = 3 \pm 20\sqrt{5}$
(D) $x = 3 \pm \sqrt{5}$

Answers

1. D	5. A
2. C	6. 4
3. 5	7. B
4. 5	8. D

Full Solutions

4.

* Algebraic solution: We are being asked to factor $x^2 + 2x - 35$. But we are also given that one of the factors $(x + 7)$. Since $\frac{-35}{7} = -5$, the other factor must be $(x - 5)$, and so $b = \mathbf{5}$.

Notes: (1) On the SAT, an expression of the form $x^2 + bx + c$ will usually factor as $(x + m)(x + n)$ where m and n are integers and $m \cdot n = c$.

In this problem, $c = -35$ and $m = 7$. So $n = \frac{-35}{7} = -5$.

(2) A **binomial** has two terms. For example, the two terms of $(x + 7)$ are x and 7. The two terms of $(x - 5)$ are x and -5.

Solution by picking a number: Let's choose a value for x, say $x = 0$. Then $x^2 + 2x - 35 = -35$, $(x + 7) = 7$, and $(x - b) = -b$. So we have $-35 = 7(-b) = -7b$, and so $b = \frac{-35}{-7} = \mathbf{5}$.

Note: By picking the number $x = 0$, we have changed the problem to "the number -35 can be written as a product of 7 and what other number?" The other number is $-b = -5$, and so $b = 5$.

5.

* Solution using trinomial factoring:

$$16x^6 + 40x^3y^2 + 25y^4 = (4x^3 + 5y^2)(4x^3 + 5y^2) = (4x^3 + 5y^2)^2$$

This is choice (A).

Note: This problem can also be solved by picking numbers (try $x = y = 1$). I leave this solution to the reader.

6.

*Solution using the square root property: Replacing y with 4 in the first equation yields $(x - 3)^2 = 4$. We use the square root property to get $x - 3 = \pm 2$. So $x = 3 \pm 2$. So the two solutions are $x = 3 + 2 = 5$ and $x = 3 - 2 = 1$.

So $P = (1,4)$ and $Q = (5,4)$. The distance between these two points is $|5 - 1| = |4| = \mathbf{4}$.

Notes: (1) To find the points of intersection of the parabola and the line, we solve the given system of equations. We chose to use the **substitution method** here.

(2) Instead of formally applying the square root property to solve $(x - 3)^2 = 4$, we can simply "guess" the solutions, or solve the equation informally. It's not too hard to see that $x = 1$ and $x = 5$ will make the equation true.

(3) It's not necessary to write down the points P and Q. Since the y-coordinates of the two points are the same, we can simply subtract one x-value from the other (disregarding the minus sign if it appears) to get the desired distance.

(4) We can also plot the two points and observe that the distance between them is 4.

7.

* Solution by factoring:

$$x^2 + 4x - 21 = (x - 3)(x + 7) = (x - 3)(x - (-7))$$

This is choice (B).

Notes: (1) $(x - 3)(x - (-7))$ is in a form where the x-intercepts 3 and -7 of the parabola are displayed as constants.

(Technically an x-intercept is a point and not a number, but the SAT seems to abuse language a bit here, and so I will do the same).

Important note: The function can also be written $h(x) = (x + 2)^2 - 25$. This is answer choice (D). This answer is **wrong** because the x-intercepts 3 and -7 do not appear as constants or coefficients!

8.

* Let's divide through by 5 first to simplify the equation. We get $x^2 - 6x + 4 = 0$. Let's solve this equation by completing the square.

$$x^2 - 6x = -4$$
$$x^2 - 6x + 9 = -4 + 9$$
$$(x - 3)^2 = 5$$
$$x - 3 = \pm\sqrt{5}$$
$$\boldsymbol{x = 3 \pm \sqrt{5}}$$

This is choice (D).

Note: This is just one of several ways to solve this problem. See problem 3 in this lesson for several other methods.

OPTIONAL MATERIAL

Standard Form for the Equation of a Circle

The standard form for the equation of a circle with center (h, k) and radius r is

$$(x - h)^2 + (y - k)^2 = r^2.$$

Example: The circle with equation $(x - 2)^2 + (y - 5)^2 = 9$ has center $(2,5)$ and radius $r = 3$.

General Form for the Equation of a Circle

The general form for the equation of a circle is

$$x^2 + y^2 + ax + by + c = 0.$$

Example: The circle with equation $x^2 + y^2 - 4x - 10y + 20 = 0$ can be put into standard form by completing the square on $x^2 - 4x$ and $y^2 - 10y$ to get $(x^2 - 4x + 4) + (y^2 - 10y + 25) + 20 - 4 - 25 = 0$, or equivalently $(x - 2)^2 + (y - 5)^2 = 9$. See the advanced course from this series for details and more practice problems.

LESSON 20
DATA ANALYSIS

Reminder: Before beginning this lesson remember to redo the problems from Lessons 4, 8, 12 and 16 that you have marked off. Do not "unmark" a question unless you get it correct.

Scatterplots

A scatterplot is a graph of plotted points that shows the relationship between two sets of data. On the SAT the "line of best fit" is sometimes drawn over a given scatterplot.

LEVEL 1: DATA ANALYSIS

Questions 1 - 4 refer to the following information.

Ten 25 year old men were asked how many hours per week they exercise and their resting heart rate was taken in beats per minute (BPM). The results are shown as points in the scatterplot below, and the line of best fit is drawn.

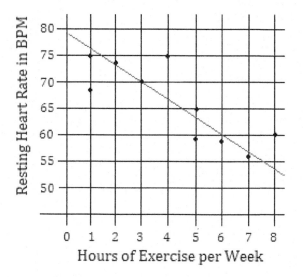

1. How many of the men have a resting heart rate that differs by more than 5 BPM from the resting heart rate predicted by the line of best fit?

    (A) None
    (B) Two
    (C) Three
    (D) Four

* The points that are more than 5 BPM away from the line of best fit occur at 1, 4, and 8 hours. So there are Three of them, choice (C).

Notes: (1) One of the two men that exercise 1 hour per week has a resting heart rate of approximately 68 BPM. The line of best fit predicts approximately 77 BPM. So this difference is $77 - 68 = 9$ BPM.

Similarly, at 4 we have a difference of approximately $75 - 67 = 8$ BPM, and at 8 we have a difference of approximately $60 - 54 = 6$ BPM.

(2) At 5, the point below the curve corresponds to a heart rate that differs from that predicted by the line of best fit by approximately $64 - 59 = 5$ BPM. Since this is not *more than* 5, we do not include this point in the count.

2. Based on the line of best fit, what is the predicted resting heart rate for someone that exercises three and a half hours per week?

    (A) 66 BPM
    (B) 68 BPM
    (C) 70 BPM
    (D) 72 BPM

* The point $(3.5, 68)$ seems to be on the line of best fit. So the answer is 68 BPM, choice (B).

3. What is the resting heart rate, in BPM, of the man represented by the data point that is farthest from the line of best fit?

    (A) 60
    (B) 66
    (C) 68
    (D) 75

* The data point that is furthest from the line of best fit is at $(1, 68)$. This point represents a man with a resting heart rate of 68 BPM, choice (C).

4. Which of the following is the best interpretation of the slope of the line of best fit in the context of this problem?

    (A) The predicted number of hours that a person must exercise to maintain a resting heart rate of 50 BPM.
    (B) The predicted resting heart rate of a person that does not exercise.
    (C) The predicted decrease in resting heart rate, in BPM, for each one hour increase in weekly exercise.
    (D) The predicted increase in the number of hours of exercise needed to increase the resting heart rate by one BPM.

* The slope of the line is the $\frac{\text{change in predicted heart rate}}{\text{change in hours of exercise}}$. If we make the denominator a 1 hour increase, then the fraction is the change in predicted heart rate per 1 hour increase. Since the line is moving downward from left to right, we can replace "change" in the numerator by "decrease." So the answer is choice (C).

*Note: Recall that the slope of a line is

$$\text{Slope} = m = \frac{\text{rise}}{\text{run}} = \frac{\text{change in vertical distance}}{\text{change in horizontal distance}}$$

In this problem the change in vertical distance is the change in resting heart rate, in BPM, and the change in horizontal distance is the change in hours of exercise per week.

Scatterplot Classification

The following scatterplots show **positive associations**.

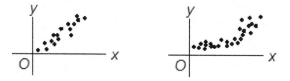

The scatterplot on the left shows a linear positive association, whereas the scatterplot on the right shows a nonlinear positive association. The rightmost scatterplot looks like it might show an exponential positive association.

Here are a few more scatterplots.

169

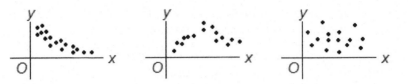

The leftmost scatterplot shows a nonlinear (possibly exponential) **negative association**, whereas the other two show **no association**.

LEVEL 3: DATA ANALYSIS

5. Which of the following graphs best shows a strong negative association between x and y ?

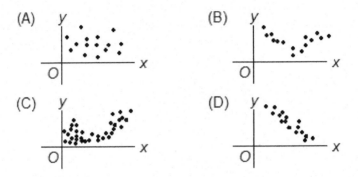

* Only the scatterplot in choice (D) is continually moving downward from left to right. So the answer is choice (D).

Other Graph Types

Several other types of graphs may appear on the SAT such as bar graphs, line graphs, circle graphs, and histograms. Here is an example of an SAT math problem involving a line graph.

LEVEL 2: PROBLEM SOLVING AND DATA

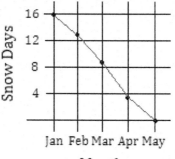

Month

6. The line graph above shows the average number of days that it snows at least 0.1 inch in Buffalo, NY from January to May. According to the graph, approximately what was the greatest decrease in the number of snow days from one month to the next month?

    (A) 2
    (B) 3
    (C) 4
    (D) 6

* The greatest decrease occurs from March to April. It is approximately $9 - 3 = 6$, choice (D).

Note: The decrease from Jan to Feb is approximately $16 - 13 = 3$.

The decrease from Feb to Mar is approximately $13 - 9 = 4$.

The decrease from Mar to Apr is approximately $9 - 3 = 6$.

The decrease from Apr to May is approximately $3 - 0 = 3$.

Now try to solve each of the following problems. The answers to these problems, followed by full solutions are at the end of this lesson. **Do not** look at the answers until you have attempted these problems yourself. Please remember to mark off any problems you get wrong.

LEVEL 3: DATA ANALYSIS

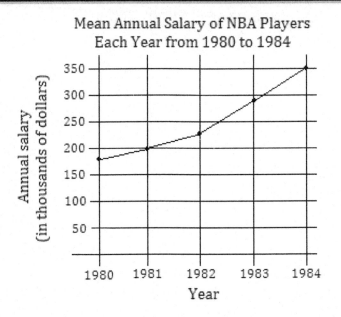

Mean Annual Salary of NBA Players
Each Year from 1980 to 1984

7. According to the line graph above, the mean annual salary of an NBA player in 1981 was what fraction of the mean annual salary of an NBA player in 1984 ?

LEVEL 4: DATA ANALYSIS

8. Which scatterplot shows a relationship that is modeled with the equation $y = ab^x$, where $a > 0$ and $0 < b < 1$?

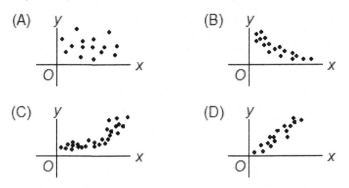

172

Percent Carbohydrate in Four Foods

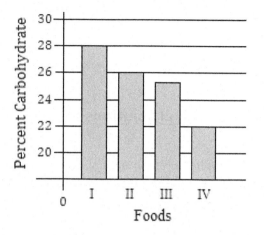

9. * The graph above shows the amount of carbohydrate supplied by four different foods, I, II, III, and IV, as a percentage of their total weights. The cost of 20 ounces of foods I, II, III, and IV, are $4.00, $3.50, $3.00, and $2.75, respectively. Which of the four foods supplies the most carbohydrate per dollar?

    (A) I

    (B) II

    (C) III

    (D) IV

SURVEY RESULTS

10. The circle graph above shows the distribution of responses to a survey in which a group of people were asked how often they donate to charity. What fraction of those surveyed reported that they donate at least yearly?

173

Answers

1. C	6. D
2. B	7. 4/7 or .571
3. C	8. B
4. C	9. C
5. D	10. 3/4 or .75

Full Solutions

7.

* According to the graph the mean annual salary of an NBA player in 1981 was $200,000 and the mean annual salary of an NBA player in 1984 was $350,000. So the answer is $\frac{200,000}{350,000} = $ **4/7 or .571**.

8.

* Choices (B) and (C) have the basic shape of exponential graphs. Choice (B) has a base between 0 and 1, whereas choice (C) has a base greater than 1. So the answer is choice (B).

9.

* 20 ounces of Food I has $.28 \cdot 20 = 5.6$ ounces of carbohydrate. Since 20 ounces of Food I costs $4.00, it has $\frac{5.6}{4} = 1.4$ ounces of carbohydrate per dollar.

20 ounces of Food II has $.26 \cdot 20 = 5.2$ ounces of carbohydrate. Since 20 ounces of Food II costs $3.50, it has $\frac{5.2}{3.5} \approx 1.49$ ounces of carbohydrate per dollar.

20 ounces of Food III has $.25 \cdot 20 = 5$ ounces of carbohydrate. Since 20 ounces of Food III costs $3.00, it has $\frac{5}{3} \approx 1.67$ ounces of carbohydrate per dollar.

20 ounces of Food IV has $.22 \cdot 20 = 4.4$ ounces of carbohydrate. Since 20 ounces of Food IV costs $2.75, it has $\frac{4.4}{2.75} = 1.6$ ounces of carbohydrate per dollar.

So it follows that Food III supplies the most carbohydrate per dollar, choice (C).

Notes: (1) 28% can be written either as the decimal .28 or the fraction $\frac{28}{100}$ (which can be reduced to $\frac{7}{25}$ if you wish).

To change a percent to a decimal, simply divide by 100, or equivalently, move the decimal point two places to the left, adding in zeros if necessary.

To change a percent to a fraction, simply place the number in front of the percent symbol (%) over 100.

(2) To take 28% of 20, we simply multiply the decimal .28 or the fraction $\frac{28}{100} = \frac{7}{25}$ by 20.

$$.28 \cdot 20 = 5.6 \quad \text{or} \quad \frac{28}{100} \cdot 20 = \frac{28}{5} = 5.6.$$

(3) We are given that 20 ounces of Food I costs $4.00. It follows from note (2) that Food I has 5.6 ounces of carbohydrate per $4.00. To see how much carbohydrate it has per dollar, we can set up a ratio.

carbohydrate	5.6	x
dollars	4	1

Now draw in the division symbols and equal sign, cross multiply and divide the corresponding ratio to find the unknown quantity x.

$$\frac{5.6}{4} = \frac{x}{1}$$
$$4x = 5.6 \cdot 1$$
$$x = \frac{5.6}{4} = 1.4$$

(4) We can do the same as we did in notes (1), (2), and (3) for the other three Foods.

10.
* "At least yearly" means yearly, monthly, or weekly. So the answer is $\frac{42+20+13}{100} = \frac{75}{100} =$ **3/4 or .75**.

LESSON 21
HEART OF ALGEBRA

Reminder: Before beginning this lesson remember to redo the problems from Lessons 1, 5, 9, 13 and 17 that you have marked off. Do not "unmark" a question unless you get it correct.

Isolating a Variable in an Equation

On the SAT you will sometimes be asked to solve for one variable in terms of others. Here is a simple example.

LEVEL 1: HEART OF ALGEBRA

$$C = \frac{5}{9}(F - 32)$$

1. The formula above shows how a temperature F, measured in degrees Fahrenheit, relates to a temperature C, measured in degrees Celsius. Which of the following gives F in terms of C ?

   (A) $F = \frac{5}{9}(C - 32)$

   (B) $F = \frac{9}{5}C + 32$

   (C) $F = \frac{9}{5}(C - 32)$

   (D) $F = \frac{9}{5}(C + 32)$

* Algebraic solution: To get F by itself we first multiply each side of the equation by $\frac{9}{5}$ to get $\frac{9}{5}C = F - 32$. We then add 32 to each side of the equation to get $\frac{9}{5}C + 32 = F$, or equivalently, $F = \frac{9}{5}C + 32$, choice (B).

Interpreting Algebraic Expressions

You will also need to be able to interpret what the coefficients and constants represent in algebraic expressions. Here is a straightforward example of this.

LEVEL 2: HEART OF ALGEBRA

$$T = 25 + 3c$$

2. The equation above is used to model the number of chirps, c, made by a certain species of cricket in one minute, and the temperature, T, in degrees Fahrenheit. According to this model, what is the meaning of the number 3 in the equation.

  (A) If a cricket chirps three more times in one minute, then the temperature, in Fahrenheit, will be one degree higher.
  (B) If a cricket chirps three fewer times in one minute, then the temperature, in Fahrenheit, will be one degree higher.
  (C) If a cricket chirps one more time in one minute, then the temperature, in Fahrenheit, will be three degrees higher.
  (D) If a cricket chirps one fewer time in one minute, then the temperature, in Fahrenheit, will be three degrees higher.

* **Algebraic solution:** The equation is linear with a slope of $3 = \frac{3}{1}$. This means that an increase in c by 1 unit corresponds to an increase in T by 3 units. This is choice (C).

Notes: (1) In the equation $T = 25 + 3c$, we are thinking of c as the **independent variable**, and T as the **dependent variable**. In other words, we input a value for c, and we get a T value as an output.

For example, if the input is $c = 2$ chirps, then the output is a temperature of $T = 25 + 3 \cdot 2 = 31°$ Farenheit.

(2) Recall that the slope of a line is

$$\text{Slope} = m = \frac{\text{change in the dependent variable}}{\text{change in the independent variable}} = \frac{\text{change in } T}{\text{change in } c}$$

(3) The **slope-intercept form of an equation of a line** is $y = mx + b$ where m is the slope of the line.

The given equation can be written $T = 3c + 25$, and we see that the slope is $m = 3 = \frac{3}{1}$.

(4) Combining notes (2) and (3), we see that a change in c by 1 unit corresponds to a change in T by 3 units.

(5) Since the sign of 3 is positive $(3 = +3)$, there is a **positive association** between c and T. It follows that an increase in c corresponds to an increase in T.

(6) As an example with a **negative association** between two variables, consider the equation

$$y = -3x + 25$$

In this equation the slope of the linear equation is $-3 = -\frac{3}{1}$. A change in x by 1 unit corresponds to a change in y by 3 units, but this time an increase in x corresponds to a *decrease* in y.

Solution by picking numbers: If $c = 1$, then $T = 25 + 3 = 28$. If $c = 2$, then $T = 25 + 3 \cdot 2 = 25 + 6 = 31$. So when the number of chirps increases by 1, the number of degrees increases by 3, choice (C).

Setting Up Algebraic Expressions

You will also need to be able to change "real world" situations into algebraic expressions. Sometimes you will need to recognize the correct setup, and sometimes you will need to solve equations. Here is an example where you simply need to recognize how to set up the expression.

LEVEL 1: HEART OF ALGEBRA

3. A caterer is hired to provide food for a private party consisting of 20 businessmen. She will be paid $80 per hour and an additional $40 tip if she serves all the food on time. If the caterer serves all the food on time, which of the following expressions can be used to determine how much the caterer earns, in dollars?

    (A) $40x + (80 + 20)$, where x is the number of businessmen
    (B) $(80 + 20)x + 40$, where x is the number of businessmen
    (C) $40x + 80$, where x is the number of hours
    (D) $80x + 40$, where x is the number of hours

* Algebraic solution: The caterer is being paid 80 dollars per hour, and she is working an unknown number of hours. So we let x be the number of hours that the caterer is working. It follows that she makes $80x$ dollars, not including her tip. When we add in the 40 dollar tip, we see that the caterer will have earned a total of $80x + 40$ dollars, where x is the number of hours she worked, choice (D).

Notes: (1) Disregarding her tip, the caterer makes 80 dollars for 1 hour, $80 \cdot 2 = 160$ dollars for two hours, $80 \cdot 3 = 240$ dollars for 3 hours, and so on.

Following this pattern, we see that in general the caterer makes $80 \cdot x$ dollars, where x is the number of hours she worked.

(2) Don't forget to add in the tip of 40 dollars at the end to get a total of $80 \cdot x + 40$ dollars.

(3) The number of businessmen is not relevant in this problem. The caterer is being paid per hour, independent of the number of people at the party.

If instead she was being paid 80 dollars per businessman, then she would have been paid a fixed amount of $80 \cdot 20 = 1600$ dollars.

Solution by picking a number: Let's choose a value for x, say $x = 2$. This means that the caterer worked for 2 hours. Since she makes $80 per hour, she made $80 \cdot 2 = 160$ dollars before receiving her tip. Since the caterer served all the food on time, she gets her tip of $40. So the caterer earned a total of $160 + 40 = $ **200** dollars.

Put a nice big dark circle around **200** so you can find it easier later. We now substitute $x = 2$ into each answer choice:

(A) $40 \cdot 2 + (80 + 20) = 80 + 100 = 180$
(B) $(80 + 20) \cdot 2 + 40 = 100 \cdot 2 + 40 = 200 + 40 = 240$
(C) $40 \cdot 2 + 80 = 80 + 80 = 160$
(D) $80 \cdot 2 + 40 = 160 + 40 = 200$

Since (A), (B), and (C) each came out incorrect, the answer is choice (D).

Important note: (D) is **not** the correct answer simply because it is equal to 200. It is correct because all three of the other choices are **not** 200. **You absolutely must check all four choices!**

Remark: All of the above computations can be done in a single step with your calculator (if a calculator is allowed for this problem).

Try to solve each of the following problems. The answers to these problems, followed by full solutions are at the end of this lesson. **Do not** look at the answers until you have attempted these problems yourself. Please remember to mark off any problems you get wrong.

LEVEL 1: HEART OF ALGEBRA

4. Which of the following mathematical expressions is equivalent to the verbal expression "A number, c, squared is 52 more than the product of c and 11"?

   (A) $2c = 52 + 11c$
   (B) $2c = 52c + 11c$
   (C) $c^2 = 52 - 11c$
   (D) $c^2 = 52 + 11c$

5. A supermarket sells protein cookies individually and in packs of 12. During a certain week, the supermarket sold a total of 315 protein cookies, of which 51 were sold individually. Which expression gives the number of packs of cookies sold during that week?

   (A) $\frac{315}{12} + 51$
   (B) $\frac{315}{12} - 51$
   (C) $\frac{315+51}{12}$
   (D) $\frac{315-51}{12}$

LEVEL 2: HEART OF ALGEBRA

$$50t + 3c = 300$$

6. Robert is playing blackjack at a casino. The equation above can be used to model the number of chips, c, that Robert still has in his possession t hours after he begins playing. What does it mean that $t = 0, c = 100$ is a solution to this equation?

   (A) Robert is losing 10 chips per hour.
   (B) It would take 100 hours for Robert to have 300 chips.
   (C) Robert can play for 100 hours before losing all his chips.
   (D) Robert begins playing with 100 chips.

180

$$A = P\frac{r(1+r)^n}{(1+r)^n - 1}$$

7. The formula above gives the payment amount per period P needed to pay off an amortized loan of P dollars at r percent annual interest with a total of n payments. Which of the following gives P in terms of A, r, and n.

(A) $P = rA$

(B) $P = (1+r)^n A$

(C) $P = A\frac{(1+r)^n - 1}{r(1+r)^n}$

(D) $P = A\frac{r(1+r)^n}{(1+r)^n - 1}$

LEVEL 3: HEART OF ALGEBRA

8. 28 male lions and 172 female lions are living in a 500 acre conservation enclosure. If 35 more male lions are introduced into the enclosure, how many more female lions must be introduced so that $\frac{6}{7}$ of the total number of lions in the enclosure are female?

9. The number of stuffed animals, q, that a toy company can sell per week at a price of p dollars is given by $q = 500 - 23p$. What is the meaning of the value 500 in this equation?

(A) 500 dollars is the maximum that someone would pay for a stuffed animal.

(B) 500 people per week would take a stuffed animal for free.

(C) If the price of a stuffed animal is decreased by 1 dollar, then 500 more people will make a purchase.

(D) If the price of a stuffed animal is decreased by 100 dollars, then 500 more people will make a purchase.

$$c = \frac{a}{a + b}$$

10. The formula above expresses c in terms of a and b. Which of the following gives a in terms of b and c ?

(A) $a = \frac{b}{c-1}$

(B) $a = \frac{b}{1-c}$

(C) $a = \frac{bc}{1-c}$

(D) $a = \frac{bc}{c-1}$

Answers

1. B	6. D
2. C	7. C
3. D	8. 206
4. D	9. B
5. D	10. C

Full Solutions

4.

* "The product of c and 11" can be written as $11c$, and so "52 more than the product of c and 11" is $11c + 52$. So we have $c^2 = 11c + 52$. This is equivalent to choice (D).

5.

* **Direct solution:** The store sold a total of 315 protein cookies, and 51 were sold individually. It follows that $315 - 51$ were sold in packs of 12. Therefore the number of packs of cookies sold during that week was $\frac{315-51}{12}$, choice (D).

Notes: (1) $315 - 51 = 264$ cookies were sold in packs of 12.

(2) $264 \div 12 = \frac{264}{12} = 22$ packs of cookies were sold.

6.

* When $t = 0$, Robert has just started playing. Since $c = 100$ at this time, Robert has 100 chips when he begins playing, choice (D).

Notes: (1) If we solve the equation for c, we get $3c = -50t + 300$, or equivalently, $c = -\frac{50}{3}t + 100$.

The number $-\frac{50}{3}$ is the slope of the line. This means that c is decreasing by 50 for every increase in t by 3. In words, Robert is losing 50 chips every 3 hours, or equivalently Robert is losing approximately 17 chips per hour. This eliminates choice (A).

(2) When $t = 100$, we have $c = -\frac{50}{3} \cdot 100 + 100 \approx -1567$. This shows that Robert does not have 300 chips after 100 hours, and that he loses all his chips before playing for 100 hours. So we can eliminate choices (B) and (C).

(3) When does Robert lose all of his chips according to the model? This happens when $c = 0$, or equivalently $50t = 300$. So $t = \frac{300}{50} = 6$.

So it takes Robert 6 hours to lose all his chips.

7.

* Algebraic solution: To get P by itself we multiply each side of the equation by the reciprocal of $\frac{r(1+r)^n}{(1+r)^n-1}$ which is $\frac{(1+r)^n-1}{r(1+r)^n}$.

$$A\frac{(1+r)^n - 1}{r(1+r)^n} = P\frac{r(1+r)^n}{(1+r)^n - 1} \cdot \frac{(1+r)^n - 1}{r(1+r)^n}$$

$$A\frac{(1+r)^n - 1}{r(1+r)^n} = P$$

This is choice (C).

8.

* Algebraic solution: Let x be the number of female lions that must be introduced. The number of female lions will then be $172 + x$ and the total number of lions will be $28 + 35 + 172 + x = 235 + x$. So we must have

$$\frac{172 + x}{235 + x} = \frac{6}{7}$$

We cross multiply to get $7(172 + x) = 6(235 + x)$. Distributing on each side gives $1204 + 7x = 1410 + 6x$. Finally we subtract $6x$ and subtract 1204 from each side of this last equation to get $x = \mathbf{206}$.

Note: This problem can also be solved by taking guesses for x. I leave this solution as an exercise for the reader.

183

9.

$*$ $q = 500$ when $p = 0$. This means that the toy company can sell 500 stuffed animals per week at a price of 0 dollars. In other words, 500 people per week would take a stuffed animal for free, choice (B).

Notes: (1) In the equation $q = 500 - 23p$, we are thinking of p as the **independent variable**, and q as the **dependent variable**. In other words, we input a value for p, and we get a q value as an output.

For example, if the input is a price of $p = 0$ dollars, then the output is a quantity of $q = 500 - 23(0) = 500$ stuffed animals.

(2) What if the question instead asked for the meaning of the number 23 in the equation?

First recall that the slope of a line is

$$\text{Slope} = m = \frac{\text{change in the dependent variable}}{\text{change in the independent variable}} = \frac{\text{change in } q}{\text{change in } p}$$

The **slope-intercept form of an equation of a line** is $y = mx + b$ where m is the slope of the line.

The given equation can be written $q = -23p + 500$, and we see that the slope is $m = -23 = -\frac{23}{1}$.

So we see that a change in p by 1 unit corresponds to a change in q by 23 units.

Since the sign of -23 is negative, there is a **negative association** between p and q. It follows that an increase in p corresponds to a decrease in q.

So if the price p of a stuffed animal is increased by 1 dollar, then 23 less people will make a purchase per week.

10.

$*$ **Algebraic solution:** We multiply each side of the given equation by $a + b$ to get $c(a + b) = a$. We then distribute on the left to get $ca + cb = a$. We subtract ca from each side to get $cb = a - ca$. Now we factor out a on the right to get $cb = a(1 - c)$. Then we divide by $(1 - c)$ to get $\frac{cb}{1-c} = a$. This is equivalent to $a = \frac{bc}{1-c}$, choice (C).

LESSON 22
GEOMETRY

Reminder: Before beginning this lesson remember to redo the problems from Lessons 2, 6, 10, 14 and 18 that you have marked off. Do not "unmark" a question unless you get it correct.

The Measure of an Exterior Angle of a Triangle is the Sum of the Measures of the Two Opposite Interior Angles of the Triangle

Try to answer the following question using this strategy. **Do not** check the solution until you have attempted this question yourself.

LEVEL 2: GEOMETRY

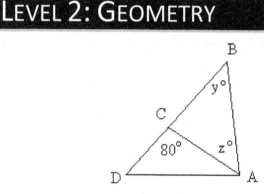

1.   In $\triangle ABD$ above, if $y = 42$, what is the value of z ?

* $80 = 42 + z$, and therefore $z = 80 - 42 = \mathbf{38}$.

Alternate method: Angles ACD and ACB form a linear pair and so are supplementary. So angle ACB has measure $180 - 80 = 100$ degrees. Since the angle measures of a triangle add up to 180 degrees, it follows that $z = 180 - 42 - 100 = \mathbf{38}$.

Move the Sides of a Figure Around

A seemingly difficult geometry problem can sometimes be made much easier by moving the sides of the figure around.

Try to answer the following question using this strategy. **Do not** check the solution until you have attempted this question yourself.

LEVEL 2: GEOMETRY

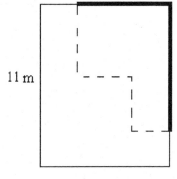

6 m

Note: Figure not drawn to scale.

2.   What is the perimeter, in meters, of the figure above?

* Recall that to compute the perimeter of the figure we need to add up the lengths of all 8 line segments in the figure. We "move" the two smaller horizontal segments up and the two smaller vertical segments to the right as shown below.

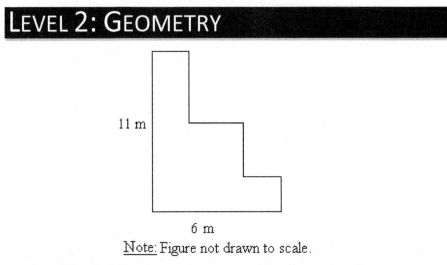

6 m

Note: Figure not drawn to scale.

Note that the "bold" length is equal to the "dashed" length. Thus, the perimeter is

$$(2)(11) + (2)(6) = 22 + 12 = \textbf{34}.$$

The Triangle Rule

The triangle rule states that the length of the third side of a triangle is between the sum and difference of the lengths of the other two sides.

Try to answer the following question using this strategy. **Do not** check the solution until you have attempted this question yourself.

LEVEL 5: GEOMETRY

3. If x is an integer greater than 7, how many different triangles are there with sides of length 4, 6 and x ?

    (A) One
    (B) Two
    (C) Three
    (D) Four

The triangle rule tells us that $6 - 4 < x < 6 + 4$. That is, $2 < x < 10$. Since x is an integer greater than 7, x can be 8 or 9. So there are **two** possibilities, choice (B).

You're doing great! Let's just practice a bit more. Try to solve each of the following problems. The answers to these problems, followed by full solutions are at the end of this lesson. **Do not** look at the answers until you have attempted these problems yourself. Please remember to mark off any problems you get wrong.

LEVEL 2: GEOMETRY

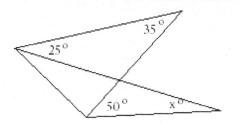

4. In the figure above, what is the value of x ?

LEVEL 3: GEOMETRY

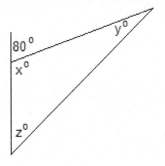

5. In the figure above, one side of a triangle is extended. Which of the following is true?

    (A) $y = 80$
    (B) $z = 80$
    (C) $z - y = 80$
    (D) $y + z = 80$

LEVEL 5: GEOMETRY

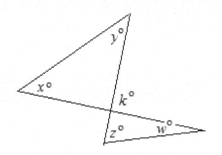

6. In the figure above, what is the average of x, y, z and w in terms of k ?

    (A) $\dfrac{k}{4}$

    (B) $\dfrac{k}{2}$

    (C) k

    (D) $2k$

7. The lengths of the sides of a triangle are x, 9, and 17, where x is the shortest side. If the triangle is not isosceles, what is a possible value of x ?

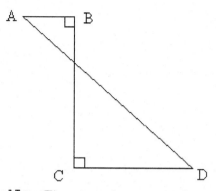

Note: Figure not drawn to scale.

8. In the figure above, $AB = 4$, $BC = 24$, and $AD = 26$. What is the length of line segment CD?

Answers

1. 38	5. D
2. 34	6. B
3. B	7. $8 < x < 9$
4. 10	8. 6

Full Solutions

4.

* The unlabeled angle in the upper triangle has measure

$$180 - 25 - 35 = 120 \text{ degrees.}$$

Thus, the unlabeled angle in the lower triangle also has measure 120 degrees (vertical angles have the same measure). So

$$x = 180 - 120 - 50 = \textbf{10}.$$

Remark: Whenever a pair of lines intersects, two pairs of **vertical angles** are formed. These are the angles that are directly across from each other. Vertical angles are **congruent**, i.e. they have the same measure.

189

5.

* The measure of an exterior angle of a triangle is the sum of the measures of the two opposite interior angles of the triangle. So $80 = y + z$, choice (D).

6.

* $k = x + y$, $k = z + w$, and so $x + y + z + w = 2k$. The average of x, y, z and w is $\frac{x+y+z+w}{4} = \frac{2k}{4} = \frac{k}{2}$, choice (B).

Remark: Note that the angle labeled k is an exterior angle of both triangles.

7.

* **Solution using the triangle rule:** By the triangle rule we have $17 - 9 < x < 17 + 9$. That is, $8 < x < 26$. Since x is the shortest side, $x < 9$. So we must choose a number between 8 and 9. Therefore we can grid in **8. 1**.

Note: We can grid in any decimal or improper fraction between 8 and 9, but be careful. Both 8 and 9 will be marked **wrong**.

8.

* The problem becomes much simpler if we "move" BC to the left and AB to the bottom as shown below.

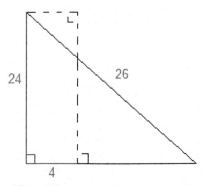

Note: Figure not drawn to scale.

We now have a single right triangle and we can either use the Pythagorean Theorem, or better yet notice that $26 = (13)(2)$ and $24 = (12)(2)$. Thus, the other leg of the triangle is $(5)(2) = 10$. So we see that CD must have length $10 - 4 = 6$.

Remark: If we didn't notice that this was a multiple of a $5 - 12 - 13$ triangle, then we would use the Pythagorean Theorem as follows.

$$(x + 4)^2 + 24^2 = 26^2$$
$$(x + 4)^2 + 576 = 676$$
$$(x + 4)^2 = 100$$
$$x + 4 = 10$$
$$x = 6$$

OPTIONAL MATERIAL

Generalized Pythagorean Theorem

The length d of the long diagonal of a rectangular solid is

$$d^2 = a^2 + b^2 + c^2$$

where a, b and c are the length, width and height of the rectangular solid.

Example: Find the length of the longest line segment with endpoints on a cube with side length 4.

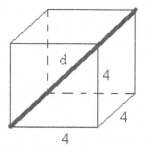

* In this problem, our rectangular solid is a cube. Thus, a, b and c are all equal to 4. So $d^2 = a^2 + b^2 + c^2 = 4^2 + 4^2 + 4^2 = 48 = 16 \cdot 3$. So $d = 4\sqrt{3}$.

LESSON 23
PASSPORT TO ADVANCED MATH

Reminder: Before beginning this lesson remember to redo the problems from Lessons 3, 7, 11, 15 and 19 that you have marked off. Do not "unmark" a question unless you get it correct.

Standard Form for a Quadratic Function

The standard form for a quadratic function is

$$y - k = a(x - h)^2.$$

The graph is a parabola with **vertex** at (h, k). The parabola opens upwards if $a > 0$ and downwards if $a < 0$.

Example 1: Let the function f be defined by $f(x) = 2(x - 1)^2 + 3$. For what value of x will the function f have its minimum value?

The graph of this function is an upward facing parabola with vertex $(1,3)$. Therefore the answer is $x = \mathbf{1}$.

Remark: Note that in this example $k = 3$ and k is on the right hand side of the equation instead of on the left.

General Form for a Quadratic Function

The general form for a quadratic function is

$$y = ax^2 + bx + c.$$

The graph of this function is a parabola whose vertex has x-coordinate

$$-\frac{b}{2a}$$

The parabola opens upwards if $a > 0$ and downwards if $a < 0$.

Example 2: Let the function f be defined by $f(x) = -2x^2 - 6x + 5$. For what value of x will the function f have its maximum value?

The graph of this function is a downward facing parabola, and we see that $a = -2$, and $b = -6$. Therefore the x-coordinate of the vertex is $x = \frac{6}{-4} = -3/2$.

Sum and Product of Roots of a Quadratic Function

Let r and s be the roots of the quadratic equation $x^2 + bx + c = 0$. Then

$$b = -(r + s) \quad \text{and} \quad c = rs.$$

Try to answer the following question using these formulas. **Do not** check the solution until you have attempted this question yourself.

Level 4: Advanced Math

$$(x - n)(x - 9) = x^2 - 4nx + k$$

1. In the equation above, n and k are constants. If the equation is true for all values of x, what is the value of k ?

* The left hand side is 0 when $x = 9$ and $x = n$. The coefficient of x is the negative of the sum of these roots, and so $4n = n + 9$, or $3n = 9$. So $n = 3$. The constant term is the product of these roots, so that $k = 9 \cdot 3 = \mathbf{27}$.

Before we go on, try to solve this problem in two other ways.

(1) By plugging in specific values for x (Picking numbers).
(2) By multiplying out the left hand side and equating coefficients.

Solution by picking numbers: Let's plug in some simple values for x.

$x = 0: 9n = k$
$x = 9: 0 = 81 - 36n + k$

Substituting $9n$ for k in the second equation yields $0 = 81 - 27n$, so that $27n = 81$, and $n = \dfrac{81}{27} = 3$. Finally, $k = 9n = 9 \cdot 3 = \mathbf{27}$.

Algebraic solution: Multiply out the left hand side (FOIL) to get

$$x^2 - 9x - nx + 9n = x^2 - (9 + n)x + 9n$$

Setting the coefficient of x on the left equal to the coefficient of x on the right yields $-(9 + n) = -4n$, or $9 + n = 4n$, or $3n = 9$. So $n = 3$. Equating the constant terms on left and right yields $9n = k$. Substituting 3 in for n gives $k = 9 \cdot 3 = \mathbf{27}$.

Now try to solve each of the following problems. The answers to these problems, followed by full solutions are at the end of this lesson. **Do not** look at the answers until you have attempted these problems yourself. Please remember to mark off any problems you get wrong.

LEVEL 4: ADVANCED MATH

$$y = -3(x - 2)^2 + 5$$

2. In the xy-plane, line ℓ passes through the point $(-2,3)$ and the vertex of the parabola with the equation above. What is the slope of line ℓ ?

3. The function g is defined by $g(x) = 2x^2 - 5$. What are all possible values of $g(x)$ where $-3 < x < 3$?

    (A) $-5 < g(x) < 18$
    (B) $0 \leq g(x) < 18$
    (C) $0 < g(x) < 13$
    (D) $-5 \leq g(x) < 13$

$$-2x^2 + bx + 5$$

4. In the xy-plane, the graph of the equation above assumes its maximum value at $x = 2$. What is the value of b?

5. For all real numbers x, let the function g be defined by $g(x) = p(x - h)^2 + k$, where p, h, and k are constants with $p, k > 0$. Which of the following CANNOT be true?

    (A) $g(7) = -h$
    (B) $g(7) = 2$
    (C) $g(0) = -2$
    (D) $g(0) = 2$

LEVEL 5: ADVANCED MATH

6. What is the sum of all values of k that satisfy $3k^2 - 27k + 18 = 0$?

194

7. If $x^2 = 9$ and $y^2 = 5$, then $(2x + y)^2$ could equal which of the following?

   (A) 41
   (B) 61
   (C) $61 - 12\sqrt{5}$
   (D) $41 + 12\sqrt{5}$

8. Let the function g be defined by $g(x) = a(x - h)^2$, where h is a positive constant, and a is a negative constant. For what value of x will the function g have its maximum value?

   (A) $-h$
   (B) $-a$
   (C) a
   (D) h

Answers

1. 27	5. C
2. 1/2 or .5	6. 9
3. D	7. D
4. 8	8. D

Full Solutions

2.

* Solution using the standard form of a quadratic equation: The vertex of the parabola is $(2,5)$. Therefore the slope of the line is

$$\frac{5-3}{2-(-2)} = \frac{2}{4} = 1/2 \text{ or } .5.$$

3.

Solution by picking a number: Let's try a value for x in the given range, say $x = 0$. Then $g(x) = -5$. So we can eliminate choices (A), (B), and (C). Thus, the answer is choice (D).

* Quick solution: g is an **even** function. So we need only check the possible values of $g(x)$ for which $0 \leq x < 3$. We have $g(0) = -5$ and $g(3) = 2(3)^2 - 5 = 2(9) - 5 = 18 - 5 = 13$. So the answer is (D).

195

Solution using the general form for a quadratic function: Using the formula $x = -\frac{b}{2a}$ we see that the x-coordinate of the vertex of the parabola is $x = 0$ (since $b = 0$). The parabola opens upwards ($a = 4 >$ 0). So the minimum value of $g(x)$ is $g(0) = -5$. We substitute $x = 3$ (or $x = -3$) to find the upper bound:

$$g(3) = 2(3)^2 - 5 = 2(9) - 5 = 18 - 5 = 13.$$

So we must have $-5 \le g(x) < 13$, choice (D).

Graphical solution: In your graphing calculator press Y=, and under Y1=, type 2X^2 – 5. Press WINDOW and set Xmin = –3, Xmax = 3, Ymin = –5, and Ymax = 18. Then press GRAPH. There is a bit of space up top, so change Ymax to 13. Now it's a perfect fit, and so the answer is (D).

Remark: We chose the window in the last solution by using the smallest and largest values that appear in the answer choices.

    4.

Solution using the general form for a quadratic function: Using the formula $x = -\frac{b}{2a}$ we have $-\frac{b}{2(-2)} = 2$. So $b = \mathbf{8}$.

Solution using calculus: The derivative of $y = -2x^2 + bx + 5$ is $y' = -4x + b$. We set the derivative equal to 0 and plug in $x = 2$ to get $-4(2) + b = 0$, or $b = \mathbf{8}$.

    5.

Solution by starting with choice (C): Let's start with choice (C) and suppose that $g(0) = -2$. Then $-2 = p(0 - h)^2 + k = ph^2 + k$. Since p and k are greater than 0, $ph^2 + k > 0$. Therefore $ph^2 + k$ CANNOT be -2, and the answer is choice (C).

Eliminating the other answer choices: This isn't necessary to solve the problem, but for completeness let's show that each of the other answer choices CAN be true.

(A) If $g(7) = -h$, then $-h = p(7 - h)^2 + k$. Let $h = -1$. Then $1 = 64p + k$, so $k = 1 - 64p$. Now let $p = \frac{1}{128}$. Then $k = 1 - \frac{1}{2} = \frac{1}{2}$.

(B) If $g(7) = 2$, then $2 = p(7 - h)^2 + k$. Let $h = 0$. So $2 = 49p + k$, and therefore $k = 2 - 49p$. Now let $p = \frac{1}{49}$. Then $k = 2 - 1 = 1$.

(D) If $g(0) = 2$, then $2 = p(0 - h)^2 + k$. Let $h = 0$ and $p = 1$. Then $k = 2$.

6.

* We divide each side of the equation by 3 to get $k^2 - 9k + 6$. The sum we are looking for is the negative of the coefficient of k in the equation, i.e. the answer is **9**.

7.

* **Calculator solution:** Taking positive square roots in our calculator gives $x = 3$ and $y \approx 2.236$. Substituting into the given expression we get $(2 \cdot 3 + 2.236)^2 \approx 67.832$. Let's see if choice (D) matches with this. We put the number in choice (D) in our calculator to get approximately 67.832. Thus, the answer is choice (D).

Remark: There is no reason that choice (D) has to be the answer. The values we got for x and y are not the only solutions to the given equations. x can also be -3, and y can also be approximately -2.236. If the answer we got didn't agree with any of the answer choices we would have to try other values for x and y (four possibilities all together).

Algebraic solution: There are two possibilities for x: $x = 3$ and $x = -3$ There are two possibilities for y: $y = \sqrt{5}$ and $y = -\sqrt{5}$
So, there are 4 possibilities for $(2x + y)^2$.

$$\left(2 \cdot 3 + \sqrt{5}\right)^2 = \left(6 + \sqrt{5}\right)\left(6 + \sqrt{5}\right) = 36 + 12\sqrt{5} + 5 = 41 + 12\sqrt{5}$$

Since this is answer choice (D) we can stop. We do not need to do the other three computations. The answer is choice (D).

8.

* **Solution using the standard form of a quadratic equation:** The function $g(x) = a(x - h)^2$ is in standard form and thus has a graph that is a parabola with $(h, 0)$ for its vertex. Since $a < 0$ the parabola opens downwards. Thus, the maximum occurs at $x = h$, choice (D).

Graphical solution: Let's choose values for h and a, say $h = 2$ and $a = -1$. So $g(x) = -(x - 2)^2$. If we put this in our graphing calculator we see that the maximum occurs when $x = 2$. Substituting our chosen values for h and a into each answer choice yields

(A) -2
(B) 1
(C) -1
(D) 2

We can therefore eliminate choices (A), (B) and (C). Thus, the answer is choice (D).

LESSON 24
PROBLEM SOLVING

Reminder: Before beginning this lesson remember to redo the problems from Lessons 4, 8, 12, 16, and 20 that you have marked off. Do not "unmark" a question unless you get it correct.

Try to solve each of the following problems. The answers to these problems, followed by full solutions are at the end of this lesson. **Do not** look at the answers until you have attempted these problems yourself. Please remember to mark off any problems you get wrong.

LEVEL 1: PROBLEM SOLVING

1. If x hours and 17 minutes is equal to 677 minutes, what is the value of x?

2. * A 770 gallon tank is filled to capacity with water. At most how many 14 ounce bottles can be filled with water from the tank? (1 gallon = 128 ounces)

3. The mean annual salary of an NBA player, S, can be estimated using the equation $S = 161,400(1.169)^t$, where S is measured in thousands of dollars, and t represents the number of years since 1980 for $0 \leq t \leq 20$. Which of the following statements is the best interpretation of 161,400 in the context of this problem?

   (A) The estimated mean annual salary, in dollars, of an NBA player in 1980.
   (B) The estimated mean annual salary, in dollars, of an NBA player in 2000.
   (C) The estimated yearly increase in the mean annual salary of an NBA player.
   (D) The estimated yearly decrease in the mean annual salary of an NBA player.

198

LEVEL 2: PROBLEM SOLVING

Paramecia present (in thousands) over twelve days

4. A small puddle is monitored by scientists for the number of *paramecia* present. The scientists are interested in two distinct species, let's call them "species *A*" and "species *B*." At time $t = 0$, the scientists measure and estimate the amount of species *A* and species *B* present in the puddle. They then proceed to measure and record the number of each species of *paramecium* present every hour for 12 days. The data for each species were then fit by a smooth curve, as shown in the graph above. Which of the following is a correct statement about the data above?

    (A) At time $t = 0$, the number of species *B* present is 150% greater than the number of species *A* present.
    (B) At time $t = 0$, the number of species *A* present is 75% less than the number of species *B* present.
    (C) For the first 3 days, the average growth rate of species *B* is higher than the average growth rate of species *A*.
    (D) The growth rate of both species *A* and species *B* decreases for the last 8 days.

5. Running at a constant speed, an antelope traveled 150 miles in 6 hours. At this rate, how many miles did the antelope travel in 5 hours?

199

LEVEL 3: PROBLEM SOLVING

6. A mixture is made by combining a red liquid and a blue liquid so that the ratio of the red liquid to the blue liquid is 17 to 3 by weight. How many liters of the blue liquid are needed to make a 420 liter mixture?

7. A bus driver drove at an average speed of 45 miles per hour for 3 hours while the bus consumed fuel at a rate of 15 miles per gallon. How many gallons of fuel did the bus use for the entire 3-hour trip?

LEVEL 4: PROBLEM SOLVING

$$S = 25.33H + 353.16$$

8. * The linear regression model above is based on an analysis of the relationship between SAT math scores (S) and the number of hours spent studying for SAT math (H). Based on this model, which of the following statements must be true?

I. The slope indicates that as H increases by 1, S decreases by 25.33.
II. For a student that studies 15 hours for SAT math, the predicted SAT math score is greater than 700.
III. There is a negative correlation between H and S.

(A) I only
(B) II only
(C) III only
(D) I and II only

Answers

1. 11
2. 7040
3. A
4. D
5. 125
6. 63
7. 9
8. B

Full Solutions

1.

Since there are 60 minutes in an hour we note that $60 \cdot 11 = 660$. So 660 minutes is 11 hours. Since $677 - 660 = 17$, we see that 677 minutes is 11 hours and 17 minutes. Thus, the answer is **11**.

* **Quick solution:** $677 - 17 = 660$ and $\frac{660}{60} = \mathbf{11}$.

2.

* 770 gallons is equal to $770 \cdot 128 = 98{,}560$ ounces. Therefore the number of bottles that can be filled is $\frac{98{,}560}{14} = \mathbf{7040}$.

Notes: (1) Since there are 128 ounces in a gallon, 770 gallons is the same as $770 \cdot 128 = 98{,}560$ ounces.

(2) We can convert between gallons and ounces more formally by setting up a ratio.

gallons	770	1
ounces	x	128

Now draw in the division symbols and equal sign, cross multiply and divide the corresponding ratio to find the unknown quantity x.

$$\frac{770}{x} = \frac{1}{128}$$
$$1x = 770 \cdot 128$$
$$x = 98{,}560$$

(3) Instead of converting 770 gallons to 98,560 ounces, and then dividing by 14, we can instead convert 14 ounces to $\frac{14}{128} = .109375$ gallons, and then divide $\frac{770}{.109375} = 7040$.

3.

* When $t = 0$, we have

$$S = 161{,}400(1.169)^0 = 161{,}400(1) = 161{,}400.$$

Since $t = 0$ corresponds to the year 1980, it follows that 161,400 is the estimated mean annual salary, in dollars, of an NBA player in 1980. This is choice (A).

Notes: (1) The year 2000 corresponds with $t = 20$. So the estimated mean annual salary, in dollars, of an NBA player in 2000 would be $S = 161,400(1.169)^{20}$. This is a number much larger than 161,400 (it is approximately 3,666,011).

(2) The function given in this problem is an exponential function. In general, exponential functions have the form $y = ab^t$. Note that $t = 0$ corresponds to $y = a$. In other words, the initial amount is always a.

In this problem $t = 0$ corresponds to the year 1980, and so 161,400 gives the mean annual salary in 1980.

Unlike a linear function, an exponential function *does not* have a constant slope. So in this problem the yearly increase or decrease in mean annual salary cannot be described by a single number.

(3) Let's compare this to the analogous linear function. Suppose for a moment that the equation given instead was

$$S = 1.169t + 161,400$$

In this case, the number 161,400 would still describe the estimated mean annual salary, in dollars, of an NBA player in 1980.

The number 1.169 would describe the estimated yearly increase in the mean annual salary of an NBA player.

4.
* The last 8 days correspond to times $t = 4$ through $t = 12$. During this time, the growth rate of both species is decreasing. So the answer is choice (D).

Notes: (1) $300 = 100 + 2 \cdot 100$, and therefore 300 is 200% greater than 100. This eliminates choice (A).

(2) We can also use the percent change formula

$$Percent\ Change = \frac{Change}{Original} \times 100$$

Here the Original value is 100 and the Change is $300 - 100 = 200$. It follows that $Percent\ Change = \frac{200}{100} \times 100 = 200\%$.

(3) To eliminate choice (B) we can use the percent change formula again with Original value 300 and Change $300 - 100 = 200$:

$$Percent\ Change = \frac{200}{300} \times 100 = \frac{200}{3} = 66\frac{2}{3}\%.$$

(4) We can compute the average growth rate over the interval from $t = a$ to $t = b$, by computing the slope of the line passing through the points $(a, f(a))$ and $(b, f(b))$. That is, we would compute $m = \frac{f(b)-f(a)}{b-a}$.

For example, over the first 3 days, the average growth rate of species A is approximately $\frac{400-100}{3-0} = \frac{300}{3} = 100$ paramecia per day. The two points we used here were $(0,100)$ and $(3,400)$.

Similarly, over the first 3 days, the average growth rate of species B is approximately $\frac{350-300}{3-0} = \frac{50}{3} = 16\frac{2}{3}$ paramecia per day. The two points we used here were $(0,300)$ and $(3,350)$.

This eliminates choice (C).

(5) It should be noted that we do not actually need to compute the growth rates to determine which growth rate is higher. We can simply look at the "steepness" of the two curves. An easy way to do this is to draw a "tangent line" to each curve at the point where we wish to examine the growth rate. Here is an example of such an analysis at $t = 2$:

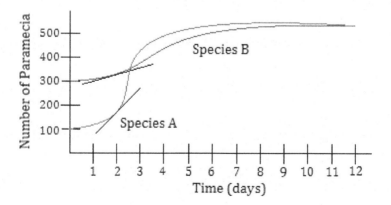

Notice that the tangent line for species A rises faster than the tangent line for species B. This shows that species A is growing faster than species B at time $t = 2$.

203

(6) We can use a similar analysis as we did in note 5 to see that the growth rate is decreasing for each species between times $t = 4$ and $t = 12$. Here as an example of such an analysis for Species B:

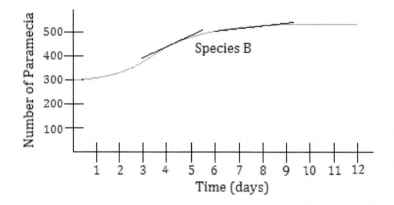

Notice that the tangent line at time $t = 4$ is steeper then the tangent line at time $t = 8$. This suggests that the growth rate of species B is decreasing from $t = 4$ to $t = 12$.

5.

Solution by setting up a ratio: We identify 2 key words. Let's choose "miles" and "hours."

miles	150	x
hours	6	5

We now find x by cross multiplying and dividing.

$$\frac{150}{6} = \frac{x}{5}$$
$$750 = 6x$$
$$x = \frac{750}{6} = \mathbf{125}.$$

Alternate solution: Using $d = r \cdot t$ (distance = rate · time), we have

$$150 = r \cdot 6$$
$$r = \frac{150}{6} = 25 \text{ mph}$$

Using $d = r \cdot t$ again, we have $d = 25 \cdot 5 = \mathbf{125}$.

* **Mental math:** 150 miles in 6 hours is 25 miles per hour (divide 150 by 6). Thus, the cheetah travelled $5 \cdot 25 = \mathbf{125}$ miles in 5 hours.

204

6.

* We can represent the number of liters of red liquid by $17x$ and the number of liters of blue liquid by $3x$ for some number x. Then the total amount of liquid is $20x$ which must be equal to 420. $20x = 420$ implies that $x = \frac{420}{20} = 21$. Since we want the number of liters of blue liquid, we need to find $3x$. This is $3(21) = \mathbf{63}$.

Important note: After you find x make sure you look at what the question is asking for. A common error is to give an answer of 21. But the amount of blue liquid is **not** equal to x. It is equal to $3x$!

Alternate solution: We set up a ratio of the amount of blue liquid to the total liquid.

blue liquid	3	x
total liquid	20	420

$$\frac{3}{20} = \frac{x}{420}$$

$$20x = 3 \cdot 420$$

$$x = 3 \cdot \frac{420}{20} = \mathbf{63}.$$

7.

* The bus driver drove $d = r \cdot t = 45 \cdot 3 = 135$ miles, and so the amount of fuel that the bus used was $\frac{135}{15} = \mathbf{9}$ gallons.

Notes: (1) We used the formula "distance = rate × time" or $d = rt$.

In this problem the rate is $r = 45$ miles/hour and the time is $t = 3$ hours.

(2) The bus gets 15 miles for each gallon of fuel. So the bus can drive 15 miles on 1 gallon of fuel. The bus can drive $15 \cdot 2 = 30$ miles on two gallons of fuel. The bus can drive $15 \cdot 3 = 45$ miles on three gallons of fuel. And so on.

In general, the bus can drive $15x$ miles on x gallons of fuel.

So we have $15x = 135$, where x is the number of gallons of fuel needed to travel 135 miles. So $x = \frac{135}{15} = 9$.

8.

* The slope of the line is $25.33 = \frac{25.33}{1}$. This indicates that as H increases by 1, S increases by 25.33. Also since the slope is positive, there is a **positive correlation** between H and S. So I and III are false, and the answer must be choice (B).

Notes: (1) We did not have to check II because once we determined that I and III were false, there was only one answer choice left that excluded both of them.

(2) For completeness let's check that II is true. To see this we just need to perform the following computation:

$$25.33(15) + 353.16 = 733.11 > 700.$$

LESSON 25
HEART OF ALGEBRA

Try to solve each of the following problems. The answers to these problems are at the end of this lesson.

Full solutions to these problems are available for free download here:

www.thesatmathprep.com/28Les500.html

LEVEL 1: HEART OF ALGEBRA

1. If $8y - 56 = 72$, then $y - 7 =$

2. For which of the following values of k will the value of $15k + 32$ be less than 10?

   (A) -2
   (B) -1
   (C) 0
   (D) 1

3. If $3z = \frac{y-5}{2}$ and $z = 5$, what is the value of y ?

   (A) 20
   (B) 25
   (C) 30
   (D) 35

4. If $6(x - 8) = 5(x - 9)$, what is the value of x?

5. If $k > 0$, for what value of k will $k^2 - 8 = 73$?

6. James solved k math problems per hour for 3 hours and Paul solved t math problems per hour for 2 hours. Which of the following represents the total number of math problems solved by James and Paul?

   (A) $2k + 3t$
   (B) $3k + 2t$
   (C) $6kt$
   (D) $5kt$

7. If $i = \sqrt{-1}$, then $(3 - 2i) + (-1 + 3i) =$

    (A) $2 - i$
    (B) $2 + i$
    (C) $4 - i$
    (D) $4 - 5i$

LEVEL 2: HEART OF ALGEBRA

8. If $3x + 11 = 24$, then $3x - 11 =$

$$2x - 3 = 4$$

9. Given the above equation, what is the value of $5 - 6(3 - 2x)$?

    (A) -20
    (B) -19
    (C) 29
    (D) 30

$$6 - 2c \geq 7 - 2c$$

10. Which of the following best describes the solutions to the inequality above?

    (A) $c \leq 1$
    (B) $c \geq 1$
    (C) All real numbers
    (D) No solution

11. If $x + 9y = 29$ and $x + 7y = 11$, what is the value of $x + 8y$?

12. Which of the following is an expression for 15 less than the product of z and 6?

    (A) $6z - 15$
    (B) $15 - 6z$
    (C) $(z + 6) - 15$
    (D) $6(z - 15)$

13. If $\frac{a+5}{3} = 40$ and $\frac{a+b}{14} = 20$, what is the value of b?

$$\frac{1}{3}x - \frac{1}{6}y = 7$$

$$\frac{1}{5}y - \frac{1}{5}x = 8$$

14. Which of the following ordered pairs (x, y) satisfies the system of equations above?

   (A) $(-36, -57)$
   (B) $(12, 43)$
   (C) $(\frac{101}{5}, \frac{307}{5})$
   (D) $(82, 122)$

15. * Gina subscribes to a cell phone service that charges a monthly fee of \$60.00. The first 500 megabytes of data is free, and the cost is \$0.15 for each additional megabyte of data used that month. Which of the following functions gives the cost, in dollars, for a month in which Gina uses x megabytes of data, where $x > 500$.

   (A) $60 + 15x$
   (B) $0.15x - 15$
   (C) $0.15x - 440$
   (D) $60 + 0.15x$

LEVEL 3: HEART OF ALGEBRA

16. If $4 - 3x = 2x + 11 - 7x$, what is the value of $x - 3$?

17. If $22x + 55y = 132$, what is the value of $2x + 5y$?

18. If $ab = \frac{5}{2}, bc = \frac{1}{3}, b^2 = 25$, what is the value of ac?

19. If $5^x = 26$, then $5^{2x} =$

20. If $(\sqrt{x})^k = 6$, what is the value of $\frac{1}{x^k}$?

21. What is one possible value of y for which $y < 15 < \frac{1}{y}$?

22. If $i = \sqrt{-1}$, and $\frac{(3-2i)}{(-1+3i)} = a + bi$, where a and b are real numbers, then what is the value of $|a + b|$?

23. A block is sliding down a ramp that drops 3 centimeters in elevation for every 5 centimeters along the length of the ramp. The top of the ramp, where the back edge of the block is initially placed, is at 60 centimeters elevation, and the block is sliding at 10 centimeters per second down the ramp. What is the elevation of the ramp, in centimeters, at the point where the back of the block passes t seconds after being released?

(A) $60 - \frac{3}{5}t$

(B) $60 - 3t$

(C) $60 - 6t$

(D) $60 - 9t$

$$T = 25 + 3c$$

24. The equation above is used to model the number of chirps, c, made by a certain species of cricket in one minute, and the temperature, T, in degrees Fahrenheit. According to this model, what is the estimated increase in temperature, in degrees Fahrenheit, when the number of chirps in one minute is increased by 1?

(A) 3

(B) 5

(C) 25

(D) 28

LEVEL 4: HEART OF ALGEBRA

$$ax + (b + 2)y = 57$$
$$ax + (b + 1)y = 23$$

25. Based on the equations above, which of the following must be true?

(A) $x = 11$
(B) $x = 25$
(C) $y = 11$
(D) $y = 34$

26. If $y = 13^x$, which of the following expressions is equivalent to $169^x - 13^{x+2}$ for all positive integer values of x?

    (A) y^2
    (B) $y^2 - y$
    (C) $y^2 - 13y$
    (D) $y^2 - 169y$

27. If y is directly proportional to x, which of the following could express y in terms of x?

    (A) $7x$

    (B) x^7

    (C) $x + 7$

    (D) $\dfrac{7}{x}$

28. Which of the following expressions is equal to -2 for some value of a ?

    (A) $|a - 1| - 1$
    (B) $|1 - a| - 1$
    (C) $|a + 1| - 1$
    (D) $|a - 1| - 2$

29. A small hotel has 18 rooms which are all occupied. If each room is occupied by either one or two guests and there are 23 guests in total, how many rooms are occupied by two guests?

LEVEL 5: HEART OF ALGEBRA

30. If $xy = 10, yz = 14, xz = 35$, and $x > 0$, then $xyz =$

31. If $x^{15} = \dfrac{2}{z}$ and $x^{14} = \dfrac{4y}{z}$ which of the following is an expression for x in terms of y?

    (A) $2y$

    (B) y

    (C) $\dfrac{1}{y}$

    (D) $\dfrac{1}{2y}$

32. If $2a - 8b = 5$, what is the value of $\frac{3^a}{9^{2b}}$?

    (A) 9^5

    (B) 3^5

    (C) $\sqrt{3^5}$

    (D) The value cannot be determined from the information given.

Answers

1. 9	9. C	17. 12	25. D
2. A	10. D	18. 1/30 or .033	26. D
3. D	11. 20	19. 676	27. A
4. 3	12. A	20. 1/36, .027 or .028	28. D
5. 9	13. 165	21. $0 < y < .067$	29. 5
6. B	14. D	22. 8/5 or 1.6	30. 70
7. B	15. B	23. C	31. D
8. 2	16. 1/2 or .5	24. A	32. C

LESSON 26
GEOMETRY AND TRIGONOMETRY

Try to solve each of the following problems. The answers to these problems are at the end of this lesson.

Full solutions to these problems are available for free download here:

www.thesatmathprep.com/28Les500.html

LEVEL 1: GEOMETRY AND TRIG

1. If the degree measures of the three angles of a triangle are $80°$, $y°$, and $y°$, what is the value of y?

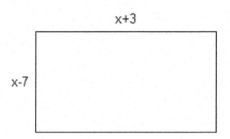

2. If the perimeter of the rectangle above is 52, what is the value of x?

3. What is the radius of a circle whose circumference is 4π?

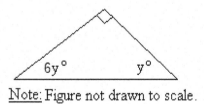

Note: Figure not drawn to scale.

4. In the right triangle above, what is the value of y?

5. In the standard (x, y) coordinate plane, what is the slope of the line segment joining the points $(3, -5)$ and $(7, 2)$?

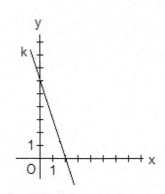

6.   What is the equation of line k in the figure above?

(A) $3x + y = 4$
(B) $3x + y = 6$
(C) $x + 3y = 12$
(D) $x + 3x = 18$

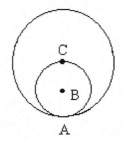

7.   In the figure above, A, B, and C lie on the same line. B is the center of the smaller circle, and C is the center of the larger circle. If the diameter of the larger circle is 40, what is the radius of the smaller circle?

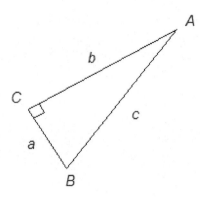

8. In the figure above, what is tan B ?

    (A) $\dfrac{c}{b}$

    (B) $\dfrac{a}{b}$

    (C) $\dfrac{a}{c}$

    (D) $\dfrac{b}{a}$

LEVEL 2: GEOMETRY

9. If the sum of the areas of two congruent squares is 72, what is the length of a side of each square?

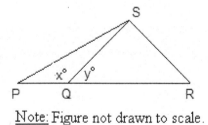

Note: Figure not drawn to scale.

10. In the figure above, point Q lies on side PR. If $48 < y < 50$, what is one possible value of x?

11. What is the area of a right triangle whose sides have lengths 15, 36, and 39?

12. A line in the xy-plane passes through the origin and has a slope of $-\frac{2}{3}$. Which of the following points lies on the line?

    (A) $(-6,4)$
    (B) $(3,-3)$
    (C) $(3,2)$
    (D) $(0,\frac{2}{3})$

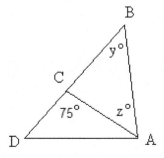

13. In $\triangle ABD$ above, if $z = 37$, what is the value of y?

14. In an xy coordinate system, which point lies in the interior of a circle with center $(0,0)$ and radius 3?

    (A) $(1,-3)$
    (B) $(-1,-2)$
    (C) $(-3,1)$
    (D) $(0,3)$

LEVEL 3: GEOMETRY AND TRIG

15. The sum of the areas of two squares is 89. If the sides of both squares have integer lengths, what is the least possible value for the length of a side of the smaller square?

Note: Figure not drawn to scale.

16. In the triangle above, x and y are integers. If $41 < x < 43$, what is one possible value of y?

17. The volume of a right circular cylinder is 1331π cubic centimeters. If the height and base radius of the cylinder are equal, what is the base diameter of the cylinder?

Note: Figure not drawn to scale.

18. In right triangle ABC above, what is the length of side AC ?

19. Which of the following equations represents a line that is perpendicular to the line with equation $y = -2x - 3$?

    (A) $2x + 3y = 1$
    (B) $2x + y = 1$
    (C) $4x - 8y = 1$
    (D) $6x - 3y = 1$

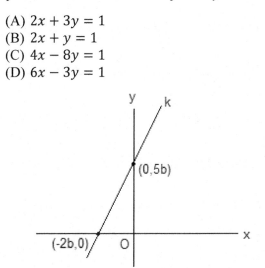

20. In the figure above, what is the slope of line k?

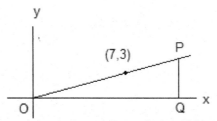

21. Line k (not shown) passes through O and intersects PQ between P and Q. What is one possible value of the slope of line k?

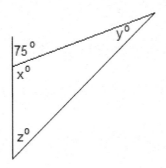

22. In the figure above, one side of a triangle is extended. Which of the following is true?

(A) $y = 75$
(B) $z = 75$
(C) $z - y = 75$
(D) $y + z = 75$

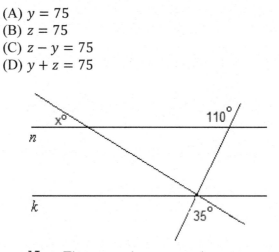

Note: Figure not drawn to scale.

23. In the figure above $k \parallel n$. What is the value of x?

218

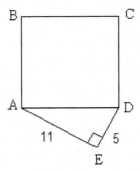

24. In the figure above, what is the area of square $ABCD$?

25. In a right triangle, one angle measures $x°$, where $\cos x° = \frac{2}{3}$. What is $\sin((90 - x)°)$

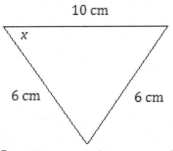

Note: Figure not drawn to scale.

26. The dimensions of a triangular block are shown above. What is the value of $\cos x$?

LEVEL 4: GEOMETRY

27. What is the area of a square whose diagonal has length $5\sqrt{2}$?

28. A container in the shape of a right circular cylinder has an inside base radius of 5 centimeters and an inside height of 6 centimeters. This cylinder is completely filled with fluid. All of the fluid is then poured into a second right circular cylinder with a larger inside base radius of 7 centimeters. What must be the minimum inside height, in centimeters, of the second container?

(A) $\frac{5}{\sqrt{7}}$

(B) $\frac{7}{5}$

(C) 5

(D) $\frac{150}{49}$

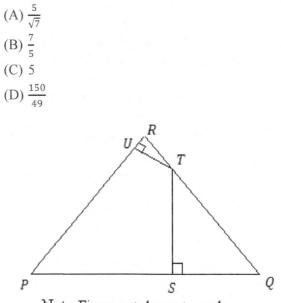

Note: Figure not drawn to scale.

29. Triangle PQR above is equilateral with $PQ = 44$. The ratio of ST to TU is $8:3$. What is the length of $\overline{SQ}$?

(A) 6
(B) 16
(C) $16\sqrt{3}$
(D) 32

LEVEL 5: GEOMETRY

30. The lengths of the sides of an isosceles triangle are n, n and 9. If n is an integer, what is the smallest possible perimeter of the triangle?

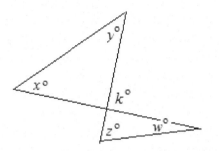

31. In the figure above, what is the sum of x, y, z and w in terms of k?

   (A) $\dfrac{k}{4}$

   (B) $\dfrac{k}{2}$

   (C) k

   (D) $2k$

32. Points Q, R and S lie in a plane. If the distance between Q and R is 15 and the distance between R and S is 9, which of the following could be the distance between Q and S?

   I. 6
   II. 17
   III. 24

   (A) I only
   (B) II only
   (C) I and III only
   (D) I, II, and III

Answers

1. 50	9. 6	17. 22	25. 2/3, .666, or .667
2. 15	10. 131	18. 12	26. 5/6 or .833
3. 2	11. 270	19. C	27. 25
4. 90/7, 12.8 or 12.9	12. A	20. 5/2 or 2.5	28. D
5. 7/4 or 1.75	13. 38	21. $0 < m < .429$	29. B
6. B	14. B	22. D	30. 19
7. 10	15. 5	23. 75	31. D
8. D	16. 96	24. 146	32. D

LESSON 27
PASSPORT TO ADVANCED MATH

Try to solve each of the following problems. The answers to these problems are at the end of this lesson.

Full solutions to these problems are available for free download here:

www.thesatmathprep.com/28Les500.html

LEVEL 1: ADVANCED MATH

1. For the function $f(x) = 2x^3 + 5x^2$, what is the value of $f(-2)$?

2. If $y = kx$ where k is a constant, and $x = 3$ when $y = 15$, what is the value of x when $y = 35$?

    (A) 6
    (B) 7
    (C) 12
    (D) 20

LEVEL 2: ADVANCED MATH

$$f(x) = x^3 + 1$$
$$g(x) = x^2 - 2x + 3$$

3. The functions f and g are defined above. What is the value of $f(5) - g(6)$?

4. Let a function of 2 variables be defined by $g(x, y) = xy + 3xy^2 - (x - y^2)$. What is the value of $g(2, -1)$?

5. If $g(x) = -3x - 7$, what is $g(-4x)$ equal to?

    (A) $12x^2 + 28x$
    (B) $12x + 7$
    (C) $12x - 7$
    (D) $-12x + 7$

6. If $g(x - 3) = 5x + 1$ for all values of x, what is the value of $g(-2)$?

$$2(x - 2)(3x + 1)$$

7. If we rewrite the expression above in the form $ax^2 + bx + c$, then what is the value of $a - b$?

$$6x^2 - 3x - 5$$
$$7x^2 + 4x + 1$$

8. If the sum of the two polynomials given above is written in the form $ax^2 + bx + c$, then $a + b + c =$

$$3(-2x^3 + 5x^2 - x + 1) - 3(x^3 - 2x^2 - 5x - 2)$$

9. If we write the above expression in the form $ax^3 + bx^2 + cx + d$, where a, b, c, and d are constants, what is the value of c ?

LEVEL 3: ADVANCED MATH

10. Let h be a function such that $h(x) = |5x| + c$ where c is a constant. If $h(3) = -4$, what is the value of $h(-6)$?

11. Let the function g be defined for $x \neq 0$ by $g(x) = \frac{k}{x}$, where k is a constant. If $g(4) = 7$, what is $g(7)$?

12. The function p is defined by $p(x) = 5x^2 - cx + 8$, where c is a constant. In the xy-plane, the graph of $y = p(x)$ crosses the x-axis where $x = 4$. What is the value of c?

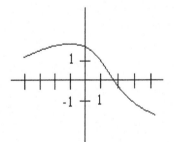

13. The figure above shows the graph of the function g. Which of the following is less than $g(2)$?

    (A) $g(-3)$
    (B) $g(-1)$
    (C) $g(0)$
    (D) $g(3)$

14. If $k \neq 0$, what is the value of $\dfrac{9(2k)^3}{(3k)^3}$?

15. If $b = 5a^3 - 2a + 7$ and $c = 2a^2 + a + 3$, what is $3c - b$ in terms of a ?

    (A) $-5a^3 + 6a^2 + a + 16$
    (B) $-5a^3 + 6a^2 + 3a - 4$
    (C) $-5a^3 + 6a^2 + 5a + 2$
    (D) $a^2 + 5a + 2$

$$3(a + b) = 4(b - a)$$

16. If (a, b) is a solution to the equation above and $a \neq 0$, what is the ratio $\dfrac{b}{a}$?

$$x^2 - 2x = 7$$

17. * In the quadratic equation above, find the positive solution for x to the nearest tenth.

LEVEL 4: ADVANCED MATH

x	$p(x)$	$q(x)$	$r(x)$
-2	-3	4	-3
-1	2	1	2
0	5	-1	-6
1	-7	0	-5

18. The functions p, q and r are defined for all values of x, and certain values of those functions are given in the table above. What is the value of $p(-2) + q(0) - r(1)$?

19. Let $\boxdot$ be defined by $x \boxdot y = x^{y+1}$. If $a = 3 \boxdot x$, $b = 3 \boxdot y$, and $x + y = 2$, what is the value of ab?

20. Let the function f be defined for all values of x by $f(x) = x(x + 1)$. If k is a positive number and $f(k + 6) = 90$, what is the value of k ?

224

21. For all numbers x, define the function h by $h(x) = 2x + 6$. Which of the following is equal to $h(6) + h(5)$?

   (A) $h(11)$
   (B) $h(14)$
   (C) $h(32)$
   (D) $h(34)$

x	-2	0	2
$f(x)$	$\dfrac{3}{25}$	3	75

22. The table above shows some values for the function f. If $f(x) = ab^x$ for some positive constants a and b, what is the value of b ?

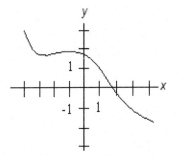

23. What is the maximum value of the function graphed on the xy-plane above, for $-4 \le x \le 4$?

   (A) -4
   (B) 3
   (C) 4
   (D) ∞

225

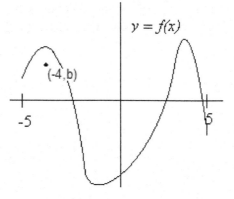

24. The figure above shows the graph of the function f and the point $(-4, b)$. For how many values of x between -5 and 5 does $f(x) = b$?

25. The function g has the property that $g(a) = g(b)$ for all real numbers a and b. What is the graph of $y = g(x)$ in the xy-plane?

    (A) A parabola symmetric about the x-axis
    (B) A line with slope 0
    (C) A line with slope 1
    (D) A line with no slope

$$(x - 16)(x - n) = x^2 - 9nx + k$$

26. In the equation above, n and k are constants. If the equation is true for all values of x, what is the value of k ?

27. In the equation $x^2 - bx + c = 0$, b and c are integers. The solutions of this equation are 2 and 3. What is $c - b$?

$$h(x) = (x - 3)(x + 7)$$

28. Which of the following is an equivalent form of the function h above in which the minimum value of h appears as a coefficient or constant?

    (A) $h(x) = x^2 - 21$
    (B) $h(x) = x^2 + 4x - 21$
    (C) $h(x) = (x - 2)^2 - 21$
    (D) $h(x) = (x + 2)^2 - 25$

LEVEL 5: ADVANCED MATH

29. Let g be a function such that $g(x) = k(x - 7)(x + 7)$ where k is a nonzero constant. If $g(a - 6.3) = 0$ and $a > 0$, what is the value of a?

x	1	6	11
$f(x)$	2	a	14

x	4	12	16
$g(x)$	3	b	15

30. The tables above show some values for the functions f and g. If f and g are linear functions, what is the value of $2a + b$?

31. For all $x > 0$, the function f is defined by $f(x) = (\frac{1}{b^5})^x$, where b is a constant greater than 1. Which of the following is equivalent to $f(3x)$?

    (A) $\sqrt[3]{f(x)}$
    (B) $(f(x))^3$
    (C) $3f(x)$
    (D) $\frac{1}{3}f(x)$

$$x^2 + 2x - 1$$
$$2x^2 - x + 3$$

32. The product of the two polynomials shown above can be written in the form $ax^4 + bx^3 + cx^2 + dx + e$. What is the value of $\frac{b}{d}$?

Answers

1. 4	9. 12	17. 3.8	25. B
2. B	10. 11	18. 1	26. 32
3. 99	11. 4	19. 81	27. 1
4. 3	12. 22	20. 3	28. D
5. C	13. D	21. B	29. 13.3
6. 6	14. 8/3, 2.66, or 2.67	22. 5	30. 27
7. 16	15. C	23. B	31. B
8. 10	16. 7	24. 4	32. 3/7, .428, or .429

LESSON 28
PROBLEM SOLVING AND DATA ANALYSIS

Try to solve each of the following problems. The answers to these problems are at the end of this lesson.

Full solutions to these problems are available for free download here:

www.thesatmathprep.com/28Les500.html

LEVEL 1: PROBLEM SOLVING AND DATA

1. The average (arithmetic mean) of four numbers is 71. If three of the numbers are 22, 61 and 95, what is the fourth number?

2. For which of the following lists of 5 numbers is the average (arithmetic mean) less than the median?

   (A) 3, 3, 5, 6, 6
   (B) 3, 4, 5, 7, 8
   (C) 3, 3, 5, 7, 7
   (D) 3, 4, 5, 6, 7

3. Joe, Mike, Phil, and John own a total of 137 CDs. If John owns 38 of them, what is the average (arithmetic mean) number of CDs owned by Joe, Mike, and Phil?

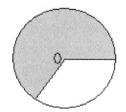

4. *O* is the center of the circle above. Approximately what percent of the circle is shaded?

   (A) 37%
   (B) 50%
   (C) 67%
   (D) 75%

228

5. If x is 22% of z and y is 37% of z, what is $x + y$ in terms of z?

    (A) $.15z$
    (B) $.43z$
    (C) $.59z$
    (D) $.81z$

6. The sales tax on a $7.50 scarf is $0.60. At this rate what would be the sales tax on a $12.00 scarf? (Disregard the dollar sign when gridding in your answer.)

7. The ratio of 29 to 5 is equal to the ratio of 203 to what number?

8. A copy machine makes 3200 copies per hour. At this rate, in how many <u>minutes</u> can the copy machine produce 800 copies?

LEVEL 2: PROBLEM SOLVING AND DATA

9. The average (arithmetic mean) of z, 2, 16, and 21 is z. What is the value of z?

10. A is a set of numbers whose average (arithmetic mean) is 15. B is a set that is generated by multiplying each number in A by six. What is the average of the numbers in set B?

11. The average (arithmetic mean) of sixteen numbers is 90. If a seventeenth number, 73, is added to the group, what is the average of the seventeen numbers?

$$15, 17, 3, 19, 2, 5, 22, 36, b$$

12. If b is the median of the 9 numbers listed above, which of the following could be the value of b?

    (A) 4
    (B) 8
    (C) 14
    (D) 16

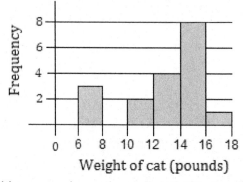

Weight of cat (pounds)

13. The histogram above shows the distribution of the weights, in pounds, of 18 cats in a shelter. Which of the following could be the median weight of the 18 cats represented in the histogram?

(A) 10 pounds
(B) 11 pounds
(C) 13.5 pounds
(D) 16 pounds

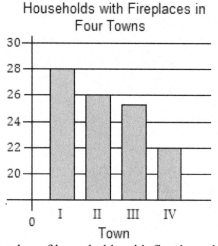

14. * The number of households with fireplaces in 4 towns is shown in the graph above. If the total number of such households is 10,150, what is an appropriate label for the vertical axis of the graph?

(A) Number of households with fireplaces (in tens)
(B) Number of households with fireplaces (in hundreds)
(C) Number of households with fireplaces (in thousands)
(D) Number of households with fireplaces (in tens of thousands)

15. * A chemist has a supply of 5.2 liter bottles of a certain solvent that must be shipped to a central warehouse. The warehouse can accept the solvent at the rate of 3 hectoliters per minute for a maximum of 8 hours per day. If 1 hectoliter equals 100 liters, what is the maximum number of bottles that the warehouse could receive from the chemist each day?

   (A) 461
   (B) 462
   (C) 27,692
   (D) 83,200

LEVEL 3: PROBLEM SOLVING AND DATA

16. The average (arithmetic mean) of nine numbers is 55. When a tenth number is added, the average of the ten numbers is also 55. What is the tenth number?

17. The average of x, y, z, and w is 9 and the average of z and w is 11. What is the average of x and y?

18. The mean length of a pop song released in the 1980's was 4 minutes and 8 seconds. The mean length of a pop song released in the 1990's was 4 minutes and 14 seconds. Which of the following must be true about the mean length of a pop song released between 1980 and 1999?

   (A) The mean length must be equal to 4 minutes and 11 seconds.
   (B) The mean length must be less than 4 minutes and 11 seconds.
   (C) The mean length must be greater than 4 minutes and 11 seconds.
   (D) The mean length must be between 4 minutes and 8 seconds and 4 minutes and 14 seconds.

19. What percent of 75 is 32? (Disregard the percent symbol when gridding in your answer.)

20. During a sale at a music store, if a customer buys one CD at full price, the customer is given a 60 percent discount on a second CD of equal or lesser value. If John buys two CDs that have full prices of $15 and $25, by what percent is the total cost of the two CDs reduced during the sale? (Disregard the percent symbol when you grid your answer.)

231

Questions 21 - 22 refer to the following information.

The graph below displays the total cost C, in dollars, of renting a car for d days.

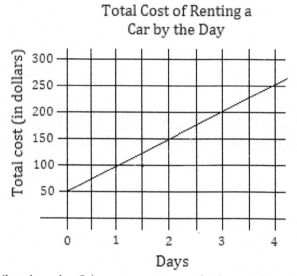

21. What does the C-intercept represent in the graph?

   (A) The total number of days the cars is rented
   (B) The total number of cars rented
   (C) The initial cost of renting the car
   (D) The increase in cost to rent the car for each additional day

22. Which of the following represents the relationship between C and d ?

   (A) $d = 50C$
   (B) $C = 50d$
   (C) $C = 100d + 50$
   (D) $C = 50d + 50$

232

23. Which of the following graphs best shows a strong positive association between x and y ?

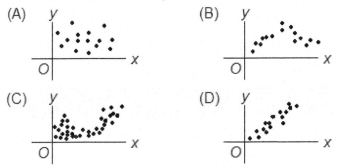

24. Daniel is drawing a time line to represent a 1000-year period of time. If he makes the time line 75 inches long and draws it to scale, how many inches will represent 80 years?

25. The ratio of the number of boys to the number of girls in a park is 5 to 11. What percent of the children in the park are girls?

    (A) 12.5%
    (B) 37.5%
    (C) 62.5%
    (D) 68.75%

LEVEL 4: PROBLEM SOLVING AND DATA

26. If the average (arithmetic mean) of k and $k + 5$ is b and if the average of k and $k - 9$ is c, what is the average of b and c?

    (A) $k - 2$
    (B) $k - 1$
    (C) k
    (D) $k + \frac{1}{2}$

27. The average (arithmetic mean) of 7 numbers is j. If one of the numbers is k, what is the average of the remaining 6 numbers in terms of j and k?

    (A) $7j + k$
    (B) $\frac{6j-k}{7}$
    (C) $\frac{7j-k}{6}$
    (D) $\frac{7k-j}{6}$

233

28. * Jessica has two cats named Mittens and Fluffy. Last year Mittens weighed 12 pounds, and Fluffy weighed 19 pounds. Fluffy was placed on a diet, and his weight decreased by 20%. Mittens weight has increased by 20%. By what percentage did Mitten's and Fluffy's combined weight decrease, to the nearest tenth of a percent?

LEVEL 5: PROBLEM SOLVING AND DATA

29. If $f = a + b + c + d + e$, what is the average (arithmetic mean) of a, b, c, d, e, and f in terms of f ?

    (A) $\frac{f}{2}$

    (B) $\frac{f}{3}$

    (C) $\frac{f}{4}$

    (D) $\frac{f}{5}$

Questions 30 - 31 refer to the following information.

743 children from the United States, aged 6 through 11, were tested to see if they were overweight. The data are shown in the table below.

	Overweight	Not overweight	Total
Ages 6-8	31	286	317
Ages 9-11	163	263	426
Total	194	549	743

30. In 2014 the total population of children between 6 and 11 years old, inclusive, in the United States was about 74.3 million. If the test results are used to estimate information about children across the country, which of the following is the best estimate of the total number of children between 9 and 11 years old in the United States who were overweight in 2014?

    (A) 3,100,000
    (B) 16,300,000
    (C) 19,400,000
    (D) 42,600,000

31. * According to the table, which of the following statements is most likely to be true about children between 6 and 11 years old, inclusive, in the United States?

   (A) The probability that a 6-8 year old is overweight is greater than the probability that an overweight child aged 6-11 is less than 9 years old.

   (B) The probability that a 6-11 year old is overweight is greater than the probability that a 9-11 year old is not overweight.

   (C) The probability that an overweight 6-11 year old is at least 9 years old is greater than the probability that a 6-11 year old is not overweight.

   (D) The probability that a 6-8 year old is overweight is greater than the probability that a 9-11 year old is not overweight.

32. A scatterplot includes the points $(1,0)$, $(2,0)$, $(3,0)$, and $(0,-6)$. The data is fitted with a cubic curve whose equation has the form $y = x^3 + bx^2 + cx + d$. If the curve passes through all four of the given points, find he value of $b + c$.

Answers

1. 106	9. 13	17. 7	25. D
2. A	10. 90	18. D	26. B
3. 33	11. 89	19. 42.6 or 42.7	27. C
4. C	12. D	20. 45/2 or 22.5	28. 4.5
5. C	13. C	21. C	29. B
6. .96	14. B	22. D	30. B
7. 35	15. C	23. D	31. C
8. 15	16. 55	24. 6	32. 5

Congratulations! By completing the lessons in this book you have given yourself a significant advantage in SAT math. Go ahead and take a practice SAT. The math score you get should be much higher than the score you received before completing these lessons.

If you found that you were still getting many problems wrong in the last four lessons, this means that you can still show improvement by going through this book again. You can also use these last four lessons to determine exactly what you need more practice in. For example, if you got all the questions correct in Lesson 25 (Heart of Algebra), then there is no need to review the Heart of Algebra lessons in this book. But if you found, for example, that you got some questions wrong in Lesson 26 (Geometry), you may want to spend the next week or so redoing all the Geometry lessons from this book.

If you feel fairly confident with the questions from Lessons 25 through 28, then it is time to move on to the advanced book in this series. The advanced book can take you right up to an 800 in SAT math.

If you decide to use different materials for practice problems please remember to try to solve each problem that you attempt in more than one way. Remember – the actual answer is not very important. What is important is to learn as many techniques as possible. This is the best way to simultaneously increase your current score, and increase your level of mathematical maturity.

I really want to thank you for putting your trust in me and my materials, and I want to assure you that you have made excellent use of your time by studying with this book. I wish you the best of luck on the SAT, on getting into your choice college, and in life.

Dr. Steve Warner
steve@SATPrepGet800.com

ACTIONS TO COMPLETE AFTER YOU HAVE READ THIS BOOK

1. Take another practice SAT

You should see a substantial improvement in your score.

2. Continue to practice SAT math problems for 10 to 20 minutes each day

You may want to purchase *New SAT Math Problems arranged by Topic and Difficulty Level* for additional practice problems.

3. 'Like' my Facebook page

This page is updated regularly with SAT prep advice, tips, tricks, strategies, and practice problems. Visit the following webpage and click the 'like' button.

www.facebook.com/SATPrepGet800

4. Review this book

If this book helped you, please post your positive feedback on the site you purchased it from; e.g. Amazon, Barnes and Noble, etc.

5. Claim your FREE bonuses

If you have not done so yet, visit the following webpage and enter your email address to receive solutions to all the supplemental problems in this book and other materials.

www.thesatmathprep.com/28Les500.html

About the Author

Dr. Steve Warner, a New York native, earned his Ph.D. at Rutgers University in Pure Mathematics in May, 2001. While a graduate student, Dr. Warner won the TA Teaching Excellence Award.

After Rutgers, Dr. Warner joined the Penn State Mathematics Department as an Assistant Professor. In September, 2002, Dr. Warner returned to New York to accept an Assistant Professor position at Hofstra University. By September 2007, Dr. Warner had received tenure and was promoted to Associate Professor. He has taught undergraduate and graduate courses in Precalculus, Calculus, Linear Algebra, Differential Equations, Mathematical Logic, Set Theory and Abstract Algebra.

Over that time, Dr. Warner participated in a five year NSF grant, "The MSTP Project," to study and improve mathematics and science curriculum in poorly performing junior high schools. He also published several articles in scholarly journals, specifically on Mathematical Logic.

Dr. Warner has more than 15 years of experience in general math tutoring and tutoring for standardized tests such as the SAT, ACT and AP Calculus exams. He has tutored students both individually and in group settings.

In February, 2010 Dr. Warner released his first SAT prep book "The 32 Most Effective SAT Math Strategies," and in 2012 founded Get 800 Test Prep. Since then Dr. Warner has written books for the SAT, ACT, SAT Math Subject Tests and AP Calculus exams.

Dr. Steve Warner can be reached at

steve@SATPrepGet800.com

BOOKS BY DR. STEVE WARNER

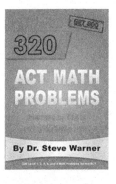

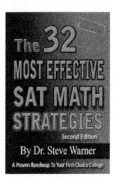

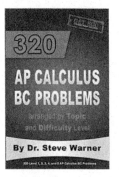

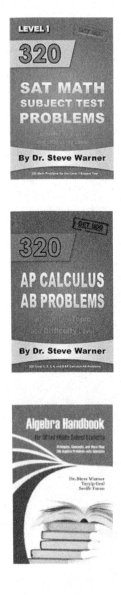

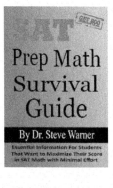

CPSIA information can be obtained at www.ICGtesting.com
Printed in the USA
BVOW05s0731050916

461145BV00024B/502/P

9 781522 856719